With gratitude to all who believed
in Moy Moy's dream and Latika's vision.

Thank you for being a part of our circle.

With love from Latika's staff and families.

Moy Moy's Circle

Suchitra Shenoy is a writer and teacher in the Buddhist tradition.

Her previous book, *Mindful Parenting: The First One Thousand Days for Parent and Baby* made Amazon India's Top Parenting Books list. Her first book, (co-authored with Pavithra Mehta), *Infinite Vision: How Aravind Became the World's Largest Business Case for Compassion*, was on Amazon's Top 40 Management Books and a finalist for the US Academy of Management's George Terry Award. It has been translated into Japanese, Portuguese and Tamil.

Suchitra teaches from the discourses of the Buddha, emphasizing practice in daily life.

When not at her desk, Suchitra enjoys being among trees and tree-dwellers. She holds degrees from Brandeis University and the London School of Economics and Political Science.

Praise for the book

'The foundational stories in Suchitra Shenoy's book of intertwined tales are about love and irrational courage. The stories also touch intriguingly on religion(s), on Indian society, and on the running of organizations. You will read the book quickly, love it deeply, and not forget it.' – **RAJMOHAN GANDHI, author and historian**

'From the foothills of the Himalayas to the classrooms of Latika, this is a deeply moving account of how one child inspired thousands to believe in a better, kinder world. Warm, wise and tender, Suchitra Shenoy tells a story that will stay with you long after the final page.' – **DUVVURI SUBBARAO, Governor, 2008–2013, the Reserve Bank of India**

Moy Moy's Circle

A True Story of Love, Disability and the World We Can Build Together

SUCHITRA SHENOY

First published in India in 2025 by Hachette India
(Registered name: Hachette Book Publishing India Pvt. Ltd)
An Hachette UK company
www.hachetteindia.com

1

All of the author royalties will be donated to Latika's challenging and joyous work with children with disabilities.

Cover design and illustrations by Harshavardhan Behura.
Illustration inputs from Kimaya Kanetkar and Freepik
The dingbat, 'Printers Ornaments One,' used in the book is designed by Michelle Dixon, as found on the website Font Squirrel.
Author photograph by Shreedhar Kanetkar

Print ISBN 978-93-5731-519-7
eBook ISBN 978-93-5731-327-8

Hachette Book Publishing India Pvt. Ltd
4th & 5th Floors, Corporate Centre,
Plot No. 94, Sector 44, Gurugram 122003, India

Typeset in Adriane Text 11.5/16.2
by InoSoft Systems, Noida

Printed and bound in India
by Thomson Press India Ltd.

For Moy Moy–

Look at what you made possible

Contents

1

Here's Someone I'd Like You to Meet

A woman from a remote village in the Himalayas is winding her way down to the city below in a crowded bus. She goes into labour and gives birth on the side of the road. The baby, born twelve weeks premature, is her thirteenth child.

The baby girl is adopted by an American woman, Jo McGowan and her Indian husband, Ravi Chopra. They already have two children and not much money. What they have are huge hearts. As Jo says, 'The baby, miraculously, against all odds, came into our lives and changed everything. She wasn't meant to survive, but she did.'[1]

They name the baby Uma (after the goddess Parvati, the daughter of the Himalayas), and affectionately call her Moy Moy (after Jo's sister).

Moy Moy, cheerful, sunny and engaging, has, it turns out, certain disabilities. At four, she's diagnosed with cerebral palsy and they learn much later, a seizure disorder. As Moy Moy's disorder progresses, she loses her ability to talk, walk, and even eat.[2] She lives as a quadriplegic, wheelchair-bound and silent. But this is *not* a story about misery. In caring for Moy Moy, Jo and Ravi create an entire loving community. 'Moy Moy was our centre,' says Jo. 'We built our world around her and everything radiated from there.'[3]

A part of that community is Latika. What started out as a play centre for Moy Moy and her siblings has transformed into a multi-service organization, a world of wonder and appropriate care for hundreds of families who desperately need it.

Situated at the base of the mighty Himalayas, the city of Dehradun is, by Indian mega-city standards, charming. It's where bureaucrats from Delhi retire to. It has a significant military presence, and is home to India's premier institute for wildlife research. A city where people know each other, nodding as you pass. Where the call of the vegetable seller or the *raddi-wallah*, still rings out as they push their carts on meandering lanes. Where your local grocery store sells not just potatoes and candy but also underwear. In 2000, Dehradun became the capital of the newly created state of Uttarakhand, and went, as someone drily put it, from one traffic light on the main road to two.

In Dehradun is Vasant Vihar, a housing community with wide roads, new mansions, old bungalows and tall trees. A large white house has a board with children's building-blocks tumbling around a name. You have reached Latika. Asha at the gate greets you, and confidently points you in the right direction. As you take a tour, two things leap out: how cheerful the people are, and how interlinked the services provided are. Latika gives love, support, insight and joy to children with disabilities, all through services undergirded by academic and scientific rigour. If you are a child with autism, Down syndrome, cerebral palsy, or developmental delays and live in Dehradun, then Latika is the place for you. You could drive up in a Mercedes-Benz, or step down from a crowded public bus: the gates of Latika are open to all.

Tom Kegelman, a friend of Ravi and Jo's from their early marching-for-peace days in the United States, laughs and says, 'In some ways their setting up a school to share with others, what they did for Moy, is totally natural; in other ways, it is magical.'[4]

This is a remarkable story hidden in plain sight.

An estimated 71 million children in India live with disabilities.[5] Sheila Josephine Chopra McGowan, known to all as Jo, seeks, through Latika, her organization, to make a better world for them. Neelam Rawat, whose child with Down syndrome attends Latika, says, 'My village is full of children with special needs – some have two in the family. There is no help, no knowledge. They are ignored. The local government school will not take the kids. Nobody plays with them. They are left in the house, in a room alone. It is *so* bad.'[6]

Latika has a strong calling to serve others. It transforms lives – of those who show up at its door for help and of those who help them. Its employees are mostly young women from impoverished backgrounds who are trained and mentored for skilled and well-paying jobs. Latika meets the needs of children with disabilities not with discipline, but with love. Not with ignorance but with skilled, trained knowledge, and not from a sense of duty but with delight. Its approach holds lessons for us all.

Numbers don't convey the magic and power of what Moy Moy inspired, but they help: By 2025, Latika offers everything from assessments and early intervention, education and therapy, to vocational training and advocacy, thus also providing meaningful jobs to 132 adults. In its twenty-five years of operations, more than 5,500 children have been assessed, taught and helped and around 4,000 professionals and more than 14,200 family members trained.[7]

Because of Moy Moy, because of Jo, thousands of people have a better understanding of the meaning of 'disability'. It is no small thing.

One learns a lot about leadership style and from talking to those who are at the bottom of an organization's hierarchy. Ashok Mamgain drives a school van at Latika. When he first joined, he was shocked to have Jo, the founder, sharing her lunch or a freshly baked cake with him. He says, 'What is inside Jo didi, is outside. She has never discriminated.'[8]

Ashok is known for his thoroughness. On the day we met, his son had broken an arm. Knowing he'd taken the day off to go to the hospital, we called to move the interview. When Ashok answered his phone, he was already at the Latika office. He made a ninety-minute round-trip for a short interview that had nothing to do with his job, on his day off, when his son was injured. You cannot buy that kind of commitment, or create it overnight.

There is a river of good cheer in all that Latika does, which is rarely seen in the working world of disabilities. There is also a belief in something deeper. Jo says, 'Whenever... the way looks dark and the task seems impossible, we think of the child whose whole existence has been a series of impossibilities and we realize... that all things are possible with faith, love and the willingness to leap into the unknown. Just leap. The net will appear.'[9]

Here is the joyous, obstacle-filled, incredible story of that leap.

2

Garam Chai, Anyone?

'I had never seen or worked with special children before. I used to think they were angry and weird. They hit people. Moy Moy changed my thinking completely,' says Harikala (Hema) Sharma. Her face lights up when talking about Jo and Moy, 'Jo didi gives so much love. Treats me like her own daughter.'

At Latika's all-staff annual meeting, the formal presentations given by each team take place over a day and a half. The final afternoon is given over to *masti* – pure, silly fun. The staff put on skits, songs, and a fashion show. Each unit within the organization tries to upstage the other: competition and camaraderie tightly interlaced. Whose Bollywood dancing is the most outrageous? Who can make the audience laugh the most? One year, as the programme began to wind down, a seven-year-old visitor, transfixed by the performances, turned to her mother and whispered, 'Ammi, Hema Aunty is in *everything*.'

She was right. Despite the internal competition on stage, it turned out that Hema had worked in, was currently at, or was 'helping out' pretty much every part of Latika.

Hema and her husband, Rajesh, are a Latika couple through and through – both work there. They used to live behind Latika's Centre for Vocational Training, and Hema was one of Moy's first caregivers.

Hema is of Nepali origin and was raised in Dehradun. 'My mother cleaned the house of the Forest Research Institute's director, so I grew up there,' she says. 'My father struggled for a long time to get a job. It was very tough.'[10] To help her parents, Hema looked for a job as soon as she finished school. She ended up at Jo and Ravi's house through word-of-mouth. As Moy Moy's caregiver, Hema became very close to Jo. The closeness was a safety net that held Hema when she needed it the most.

Hema's marriage was arranged to a Nepali man, found through the usual complex web of language, religion, caste and sub-caste. A wedding date was set, expensive clothes bought, ornate invitation cards printed. 'Then the police caught him,' Hema says. 'It was for a rape case.'[11] Her parents, feeling immense societal pressure, wanted to go ahead with the wedding: it was a matter of honour.

'Jo didi realized that I was very sad and asked what happened,' recalls Hema. When Hema poured her heart out, Jo shored her up, pointing out that Hema was over eighteen years old and therefore legally independent. She could not be forced to marry. 'She gave me the strength to stand up to my parents and say, "No,"' says Hema. 'There were so many arguments...'[12]

Jo and Ravi intervened. They spoke to both the families. The groom's side had given 10,000 rupees towards expenses incurred. How were Hema's family, barely scraping by, to pay them back? Ravi, anticipating something like this, had with foresight, carried a wad of cash. He pulled it out and repaid Hema's debt immediately. Jo told Hema to pay it back in instalments. Latika would cut a little bit from her salary every month. Ravi drafted a letter that the groom's family signed, agreeing that they would not cause any trouble, or put further pressure on Hema.

Coming from a broken engagement, even though it was not her fault, carried stigma. Hema was determined to put her head down, ignore everyone's snide remarks and concentrate on work, '*Kuch kaam karoongi, kuch banoongi.*' ('I will work hard, make something of myself.') It was very tense at home. 'My father was a drunkard,' she says. 'Then, my depression deepened when my closest brother committed suicide.' Hema came home from work and found the body. 'I called Jo didi,' she says. 'I said, "Bring a doctor and just come." I only had *bharosa* in her, no one else.'[13]

After three years as Moy Moy's caregiver, Hema moved to Latika. (This was a pattern for many of Latika's early staff. Moy would be their trainer. If they passed with flying colours, they worked at the organization.)

Rajesh joined Latika at the vocational training centre. Hema and he became friends. He supported her through all her lows. 'Everyone would tell me: "You should marry a boy like Rajesh. Look how caring he is,"' says Hema. 'But Rajesh is Christian, and my mother is a super *puja-paath waali*, so I didn't consider it at all.'[14]

Jo encouraged the bourgeoning romance. Jo and Ravi's daughter, Cathleen, started gently teasing Hema about Rajesh. Eventually, Hema's parents were persuaded. This time around, though, Hema was determined to do things differently. 'We had a court marriage,' she says. Then, with pride in her voice, she adds: 'We paid for it ourselves.'[15]

Through it all, Jo's steady, unwavering support nurtured Hema from a young, vulnerable teenager into a strong woman. Giving Hema not just a job, but creating a career-path in Latika, sending Hema for training to the big city of Mumbai, giving her housing, encouraging her to marry: there is no area in Hema's life that has not been influenced by Jo. Some might call it interference and intrusion. We are good at carving out the personal from the professional, saying – We should not be involved. With Jo it is the opposite. The personal is not walled off from the professional. Yes, it can get messy, but, for someone like Hema, it was nothing short of revolutionary.

'Jo didi gave me so much love. She is my ideal,' says Hema. '*Koshish karti hoon ki usi ki tarah bane.*' ('I try hard to be like Jo.') 'Look at me,' she says, 'I was not trained. Not famous. I was nobody. Look how well I have done! I never thought I would be a teacher to special children.' And then, with a smile that lights up the room, she says, 'God sent her to us.'[16]

It is a much-repeated family lore: a tiny premature baby that nobody wants, born on the side of a road, is left in a busy government hospital. What should be done with her? An American couple, both doctors, are studying infectious diseases there. The woman declares: 'My sister will adopt her.' (A doubly audacious move: not just swooping in to save a sickly, unknown baby, but signing up her sister's family to do so!)

Mary McGowan and Tom Synan were that American couple. Mary is Jo's younger sister. 'I am someone who takes three weeks to decide on a pair of shoes!' says Tom. 'I remember the shock of Mary saying "My sister will take her." And they decided about a baby on the spot! By the time *I* made up my mind the baby would have been eighteen years old,' he chuckles.[17] Ravi, Jo's husband, was travelling on work, and Jo had no way of getting in touch with him. Their children were young: Cathleen was three and Anand six.

When Ravi got home, weary, Jo launched into the baby's situation right away. 'Let's find out the whole story, sort out the details, think about it, and then see,' counselled Ravi. But Jo was characteristically impulsive. 'I wanted to take the baby home immediately, not leave her there in the hospital crib,' she says. 'I had never seen such a tiny, twig-like baby. All scrunched up, her legs were like a bird's. Unbelievable. Her eyes were giant, took up half her face.' Ravi and Jo did not own a car then, so Jo had wrapped the baby up and jumped into an auto-rickshaw.

Ravi opened the door at home and said, 'I *knew* you would do this.'[18]

Growing up, Moy was playful, engaging and mischievous. Her sense of humour is family legend. One story is from Moy's First Communion when she was seven years old. 'The church was freezing,' Ravi recalls. 'We were all huddled into our clothes, waiting, desperately, for the priest to finish.' Everyone was concentrating on the ceremony and the solemn, important moment it marked. In this quiet, serious and freezing occasion, Moy's young voice bellowed: '*Chai! Garam Chai!*' ("Hot tea, anyone?!")[19]

Mary, Jo's sister, remembers a time when the Chopra family were visiting the United States. All the cousins loved getting into the jacuzzi. They called it 'The J.' One night, after supper, Moy refused to get in. She said to Mary, 'Moy... J... No in. Easily bonk.' [Indicating that she got hurt in the jacuzzi, and so didn't want to get in.] 'She got her point across!' says Mary with a laugh. Moy Moy could also be a naughty handful. 'One summer, we rented a house and Jo wanted to go to Boston for the day,' recalls Mary. 'We said, Jo deserves it. We will baby-sit Moy. How hard can it be? Well, it turns out Moy can grab a stick of butter and rub it all over the kitchen, standing up on her little toes, faster than one can imagine! There was butter everywhere! I never underestimated Jo after that.'[20]

In Dehradun, Jo would bung Moy Moy into her 'throne,' a strong-wheeled stroller, and they would go on long walks. Jo never listened to her iPod at these times. 'I would chat with her and we would look at things together. It was really good for my relationship with Moy,' she says. Sometimes, Ravi would say, 'Leave Moy home with me, she'll be fine,' but Jo would consciously take her. 'I wanted Moy Moy to go out, to have the experiences my other two kids could get so easily.' Dehradun is a small city. People notice things. 'You are not even aware of who is watching. The unexpected effect was a city that got used to seeing a person with disability,' says Jo.[21]

'The idea of an adopted girl coming into our house didn't feel abnormal,' says Anand, Ravi and Jo's eldest child. 'It was the environment my parents created – people always coming home, staying with us.'[22] One of Jo's sisters is adopted, as is one of Tom and Mary's children. 'Adoption is genetic in our family,' quips Tom.[23] Anand, now a father himself, looks back and sees how remarkable an act that was, 'The decision, almost on a whim, to take on a child who will certainly have developmental problems, seems incredible.'[24]

What is it like to be an older sibling to someone with disabilities? 'I knew without being told, pretty early on, about Moy's disabilities,' says Anand. 'She would walk funny. Her sentence structures were weird. Honestly, it was tough as a sibling. That kind of difference is hard enough to cope with. On top of it, in India there is no sensitivity, no awareness... people would call out *pagal*, or stare at Moy. I think Cathleen was somehow more comfortable with it,' he admits.[25]

Mamta Govil, the current President of the Latika Board, praises both siblings. Mamta is warm, friendly and, by her own admission, very good at connecting with people. The running joke at Latika is that if six out of ten people in the world are Indians, then five of them will know Mamta! Many strands of Mamta's life tie her to the organization: Sakshi, Latika's accountant, does Mamta's tax returns. Rekha, who works at the Vocational Training Centre, cooks for her, after-hours. Jo and Mamta meet for a swim almost daily. Mamta introduced Dr Ajay Sharma, now an invaluable asset, to Latika. And, when Jo felt herself crumbling under the strain of Moy and life in its specificity, she made one phone call – to Mamta. So, Mamta's words carry a lot of weight when she says, 'You have to see Cathleen and Anand to see how they love Moy and how sure they are that they would take care of her after their parents' death. How do you engender such love among children for such a sibling?'[26]

Jo and Ravi's children, Anand, Cathleen and Moy Moy, are evenly spaced out; three years between each. Both Anand and Cathleen remember their childhood as idyllic. 'We'd play in the garden, climbing the big litchi trees,' recalls Cathleen. 'We'd make a kitchen with elaborate tea sets. There was lots of outdoors playtime.'[27] Latika was in its infancy and so Jo was able to spend a lot of time with her children.

'My mom used to take us on these picnics – there was a river that was accessible then. The three of us and all the neighbourhood kids would have a day-long picnic by the river,' says Cathleen. 'Moy and I did a lot of stuff together,' she adds, 'It was a daily connection.'[28] When the caregivers took Moy on walks, Cathleen would tag along. In the hot Indian summers, the two sisters would dig 'pools' in the garden, splashing in the one-inch-deep muddy water.

Today, Cathleen is a professor of the Hebrew Bible in the United States. Back then, Moy Moy was Cathleen's first student. Cathleen started a school in their backyard and ran it from when she was eight to about fourteen years of age: six days a week. Neighbourhood children attended, especially those who needed help in English or mathematics. Moy Moy would participate, and when bored, simply get up and run away!

Anand and Cathleen kept an eye on Moy Moy, 'If we sensed that someone was being mean, we would leave,' says Cathleen. 'There were people who stared. Anand and I would glare back and take Moy away. I always knew that Moy could understand everything that was going on around her.'[29] Anand says, 'She was a huge hit with our friends. And this was a constant theme – those who knew Moy really enjoyed being with her. The teasing and more conventional responses were from those who didn't know her.'[30]

Moy's arrival changed the kind of decisions Jo and Ravi made as a couple and in their careers. Ravi, for instance, had always been deeply involved in Indian politics, driven by the ideals of Gandhi, of building a nation based on equality and respect. His boisterous younger sister Nutan says Ravi always talked about a political career and becoming the prime minister of India. 'I once asked Ravi, "What happened to your dream of becoming a prime minister?"' she says, 'He told me, "It is not fair for Jo to handle Moy alone. For having my political dreams come true, I would have to go to Delhi a lot. Maybe even move there. It is not fair. So, for Moy, I have given up those dreams." I will never forget what he said,' Nutan remarks, her usual ebullience dimming slightly.[31]

Anand makes an interesting point about the environment created for Moy Moy. For many children with disabilities, the challenge is to introduce them to the outside world that is often harsh, hurtful and judgemental. But Anand points out that both his parents ran their own organizations, had wide social networks that were in a way filtered or sensitized to disability. It made a large, protective bubble for Moy Moy. 'My parents are both network-creators as opposed to working for others,' he says. 'So, their ability to influence or control those communities was strong. They created a situation where Moy would always be welcomed.'[32]

The welcoming, all-inclusive spirit of Jo and Ravi fuelled Latika and its specialization in disabilities. With Moy Moy's arrival, people got used to seeing tall, American Jo striding around the city with Moy in her stroller. Now, every day, Latika cares for more than four hundred children who have special needs.[33] And just like Jo and Moy Moy, the children are often taken around town, on trips and joyful adventures. Everyone learns: other children in the city, neighbours, restaurant owners, shop-keepers. 'Aware *ho gaye, abhi*,' says Hema. 'Moy *ne hi kiya hai*.'[34] ('They are now aware. Moy is the one who did it.')

Almost imperceptibly, Moy Moy's disabilities began to worsen when she was around six or seven years old. 'Getting her ready in the morning was becoming difficult,' remembers Ravi. 'She would grin when I'd say, "Open your mouth to brush your teeth" and I thought she was being difficult, but she wasn't, it was a change.'[35] Shivani, one of Moy's early caregivers remembers, 'Moy stopped speaking, she started falling down, had more seizures.' Shivani adds, 'As she grew older, she got her periods. I would change those diapers, clean her. I never felt horrible doing it. So strong was our love.'[36]

'Each phase has been devastating,' wrote Cathleen when she was eighteen. 'How can I describe the grief of watching my little sister go backwards? For me, the worst has been the fear of the unknown, having no idea what she'll lose next.'[37] Cathleen worked hard to find a silver lining at each stage. 'It was only when Moy began to lose her speech that I realized the emotional depth that can be communicated through silence. When I accept Moy as she is, everything else falls into place.'[38]

It was painful for Jo and Ravi too, to watch the deterioration in Moy Moy. They didn't realize how painful it was for Moy herself, until on one occasion when the family was in a restaurant telling Moy's childhood stories. 'Moy was enjoying it, until at one point, she burst into tears,' recalls Jo. 'She was aware enough to know what was happening to her. She couldn't express it. Normally, she never made a noise, never complained. So, it was so awful when this happened.'[39]

This incident gave Jo and Ravi a sense of the depth and complexity of Moy's situation. 'I was grateful in a way for the incident, to give us this window [into her world], but it was so painful,' says Jo. She points out how children, or even adults with disabilities are not treated with dignity. 'We don't respect them, we just move them around, don't ask them anything. And people with disabilities are like that for a lifetime. Never asked what they want, never asked what they'd like.'[40]

Even after Moy stopped talking and moving, those close to her would still feel a connection. 'I used to talk to her and Moy Moy would try to move her limbs, her eyes would sparkle,' says Shivani. 'Now, very few people know how full of joy Moy was. They don't know what a foodie she was, how cheerful. They only know her stuck in a wheelchair.'[41]

'I used to call her "Moylu,"' says Manju Subedi, another caregiver and now Latika staff member, with great affection. 'She loved *rajma* and cheese, which we would take to Latika in a little tiffin-box. That tiffin feels like a dream because Moylu was on a feeding tube for so many years.'[42]

At one point, the deterioration in Moy became so apparent that Jo gathered twelve Latika colleagues, stalwarts from the early days, for a conversation. Each had a strong relationship with Moy Moy. 'Dr Linda spoke to us and so did Jo didi,' recalls Shivani. 'Dr Linda told us that Moy may not live long. We should prepare ourselves.' Shivani is weeping now, tears streaming down her cheeks. 'We all thought, *Bhagwan*, please take one year from each of us and give it to her. And perhaps because it was asked for with *sacche dil*, that it really happened, Moy lived ...'[43]

There's a ripple of energy that changes the quiet hum of the Latika Resource Centre. A man in his thirties bounces in – curly locks flying, black eyes flashing. Think Tigger from Winnie the Pooh, but with smarts. This is Rizwan Ali, Latika's one-man legal army. His enthusiasm for his work, mischievous grin and never-say-die attitude could lead you to think that what Rizwan does is glamorous – battling legal Goliaths on behalf of the disabled. There is much truth to that. But Rizwan is remarkable for his ability to work equally hard at the small but vital victories that change lives outside court. Making sure Latika is always in compliance with the law; standing in line for ages to plead for help from the local government – all tasks that are mind-numbing but crucial for parents and children. Every now and then, though, there comes a moment that sparks Rizwan's impish creativity.

Moy Moy had just turned eighteen. As an adult with severe disabilities, it made sense for her to have a legal guardian. Everyone assumed it will be her mother, Jo. Except, what should be a routine matter of filing the appropriate forms, becomes a crisis. Jo, it turns out, is ineligible under Indian law to be Moy's legal guardian, because as an American, she holds a foreign passport. Never mind that she has lived in India for more than forty years, married an Indian, raised three children and runs a successful organization in the country. (Ravi can't be the guardian because he is a man and Moy Moy, a woman. Under Indian law you can only be a legal guardian to a ward of the same gender.)

Enter Rizwan.

'Why, actually, do you want to be Moy's guardian?' he asks Jo, popping his head into her office for a brief chat. ('Rizwan's two-minute conversations, are never for two-minutes,' Jo dryly points out.) 'Well ...,' Jo stutters, having never been asked such an in-your-face question. 'Because ... Moy Moy might need medical care and I wouldn't be allowed to authorize it. Or, I might want to take her to America, and I wouldn't be allowed to apply for her visa.'[44] Pause. Then, Rizwan, with a big grin, asks, 'What about Moy Moy? What does she want?'

All the focus thus far has been on Jo. There had been much outrage among Jo, Ravi and Latika's vast network of friends and well-wishers about how ridiculous the situation is, how if anyone *deserves* this guardianship, it is Jo, etc. Emails, phone conversations and messages expressed indignation and ire at the situation.

Rizwan's maverick brain realized that the situation was about what *Moy* wanted, not Jo. As an Indian citizen and a person with disabilities, Moy was protected by India's Constitution *and* the National Disabilities Act (the National Trust for Welfare of Persons with Autism, Cerebral Palsy, Mental Retardation and Multiple Disabilities Act, 1999, to give it its full form). With all this backing her, instead of Jo wanting to be Moy's guardian, Moy could choose to have her mother, and later, her siblings, to be her guardians; the colour of their passports did not matter. Like a flash of blue as a kingfisher darts in to nab a fish, Rizwan had figured it out. Sheer brilliance.

'I was a child labourer, without knowing it,' says Rizwan about his childhood. The youngest of eight siblings, his father was a farmer; his mother died when Rizwan was in high school. Rizwan worked all the way through school and college. 'I'd write the accounts for the vegetable seller in the market – two hours in the morning, two hours in the evening, study during the day.' Earning for his daily needs and education fees meant college took five years to finish instead of the usual three, as did his law degree. 'I worked in a drug addiction centre,' he says. 'I would be there through the night, from 8 p.m. to 8 a.m.; making sure they slept, they were clean, and that they got exercise.'[45] His sisters are home-makers, while his brothers are farmers or run small, construction-related businesses. Rizwan is the only one with a professional degree.

Rizwan came to Latika in 2008, while still a law student. 'I thought the day I became a lawyer I would leave. I was very clear.' He'd become a real-estate lawyer, make a lot of money and earn more prestige than working in the field of disabilities. Fifteen years later, he's still at Latika. '*Yaha itna freedom hain, kya karna hai, kaise karna*, ("There's so much freedom here, to choose what to do, how to do it")' he says.

Working at Latika made him realize, 'getting people their rights, legal guardianships, all this was very needed.'[46] He finds a lot of satisfaction in doing the everyday stuff. For example, filling out forms for seventy families, which allow families to get financial assistance provided by the government. At least sixty-seven of them got their certificates, which shows how good he is.

'I really like giving *peeche se* support, working from behind, out-of-court stuff,' Rizwan says. He cites the example of a woman with a child with disabilities, who went through a divorce. Her ex-husband was not paying any alimony. 'I showed her what papers to submit,' says Rizwan, 'because her child was disabled. She'd been struggling for three years, getting no maintenance. But now, I showed her with a certificate or two how they could get it done. She was so happy.'[47]

Moy Moy was the locus around which Latika grew. There wasn't an appropriate enough, welcoming enough school for Moy, so her parents started one. Other parents came with questions, desperate for guidance. Their young children had to be looked after, so trained individuals were needed.

Hema spent three years with Moy, spending the whole day with her, feeding, cleaning, playing with her, doing exercises. She would put Moy Moy in the stroller and take her to the Latika school and evening play-group. 'Jo didi told me Moy is not a *bechari*,' she recalls. 'Moy used to have fits. Didi taught me how to handle that and how to respond to strangers who stare.' Hema learnt not just from what Jo said, but from what Jo did. 'Didi went everywhere with her. The market, the shops, Latika meetings, everywhere.'[48]

The specialness of Moy Moy is something that comes up repeatedly. Perhaps it was how Jo treated Moy; but also, perhaps it was the strength of Moy's personality. 'Even among special children, Moy's special,' says Hema. 'Her face has a *khichaav* (a pull).'

After spending so much time together, Hema got to really know Moy. Even though Moy never spoke, Hema felt a deep understanding and response from Moy.

It is easy, with disability, to think of all the help and support going from the caregiver to the person with the disability. Do we ever stop and think of it going the other way around?

Cathleen, Moy Moy's older sister, writes: 'Moy forced me to re-examine the way I look at life. I tend to make quick judgements and form immediate opinions, and I love the idea of perfect order. Moy taught me that the world doesn't always work that way. People fit into multiple categories. Even though I understand this concept intellectually, I am still struggling with it in real life... The most valuable thing I have learned is that now is the only time there is.'[49]

'I would share all my problems with Moy,' says Hema touchingly. 'Whatever happened at home, my mother scolding me, all the tensions at home.' And Hema's troubles were not trivial. Poverty, an alcoholic father, a broken engagement she was blamed for, a brother's suicide, opposition to her choice of husband... It is hard to fathom from Hema's smiling face how much she has endured. Moy would listen to all this and offer, through her quiet presence, that most essential of human acts: comfort.

One can picture them in a quiet corner of the garden, Moy Moy in her stroller, Hema in a colourful kurta chatting away beside her. 'Moy would comfort me, with her eyes, her lovely smile. And then,' Hema says with a lovely smile of her own, 'I would forget all my troubles.'[50]

One of the marvels of parenting is watching independence grow. In the blink of an eye, the baby who gestured for food with a toothy grin becomes a gawky teenager, answering in mono-syllables, hunched over a phone. And then, your child is gone; off to the wider world for college or a job or to travel on her own.

For parents whose children have severe disabilities, letting go rarely happens. There's a limited pathway, if at all, to independence. 'There is no day off,' Ravi points out. As Moy Moy lost her mobility, her dependence on others grew. She needed carrying in and out of bed, she needed to be dressed, cleaned, placed in her wheelchair. The loss of control over limbs coincided with eating and swallowing difficulties.

At sixteen, each meal for Moy Moy began taking more than an hour, interspersed with coughing fits that shook her body. Even though they knew it was not their fault, Jo and Ravi were racked with guilt to see Moy losing weight alarmingly. Doctors recommended a feeding tube. In a family that relished everything from pasta and apple pie to parathas, such an intervention raised the question: how would Moy be without *tasting* any food?

A feeding tube is inserted by a surgeon straight into the stomach. One end, with a stopper, protrudes out of the body. At meal time, the stopper is opened and, through a funnel, formula poured in. Warm water follows, to clean the tube. Sounds simple, right? 'In the first few days, I would be in tears trying to work it out,' recalls Jo.[51]

Moy was fed five times a day: three times a supplement called Ensure, twice milk, and additionally, anti-convulsant liquid medicines and cough syrup. Warm water to dissolve tablets in and to flush the funnel out. A big measuring cup, small cups for medicines, a whisk to smooth the paste, spoons, a jug for the warm water and a syringe, all this paraphernalia needed for *every* meal. Sometimes food would get stubbornly stuck in the funnel. If the stopper does not get in properly, and Moy Moy coughed or laughed, the food came right out hitting Jo or Ravi in the face. (Ravi, with his characteristically dry wit, called it 'playing with her food.')[52] The tube needed to be replaced every four months. With its end sticking out of Moy's body, it looked alien.

It doesn't end there. The acids in our stomach that break down the food we eat are highly corrosive. One night, Moy's tube opened. She had a high-pain threshold and didn't cry out in her sleep. When Jo woke up in the morning, the stomach acids had leaked out via the tube and burned Moy's stomach; the scars remained for years.

Nourishment is just *one* aspect of all that goes into caring for a child with severe disabilities. The remarkable thing about Jo and Ravi is how neither *ever* draws attention to these difficulties. Jo is the opposite of a moaner. Remarking on Moy's feeding-tube routine, she says, 'We got used to it quickly. It became as simple as making tea.' Her formula for living is, 'This is FUN!' In a letter to her younger self, Jo had written, 'Fun is a flighty, frivolous word that doesn't seem to cover the gravitas of what you think you are going through right now, but believe me, fun is perfect. Fun should be your mantra, the standard by which you judge whatever else you are doing with your kids, your colleagues, your life: "Are we having enough fun?"'[53]

Shaila Faleiro, a communications expert in the social sector and mother of two, has known Jo and Ravi Chopra for decades. At twenty-one, freshly trained as a special educator, she was part of the 'gang of five' that set up Latika. She calls Ravi '*Baba*' (father), and is very close to all three children. 'Jo makes things look easy,' Shaila says. 'There is always fun and much laughter, in that house and in the organization. There was never any money, but the office team, in the early days, would go for picnics with Moy, go paddling in the river, sing songs.'[54] Along with fun, Jo puts a huge emphasis on celebration.

'It is only when you looked closely, you'd see how *hard* she worked,' says Shaila. After a full day at Latika, Jo would put Moy to sleep, and then stay up late baking a cake for someone's birthday. Moy had a caregiver, but not Cathleen and Anand. 'Jo did everything: she would cook the meals, look after the children, work.' The household also had elderly members: Ravi's mother and aunt lived there, and Jo's father came for multi-month visits. As Moy got older and less able, Ravi and Jo did a lot of picking her up, moving her. 'Moy got heavier, they were getting older, yet they made it look easy; no complaints,' recalls Shaila (when Moy Moy was eighteen years old, Jo was almost fifty and Ravi just over sixty years old). 'It was phenomenal.'[55]

Over time Moy, the young girl with the gleaming eyes and sense of fun, became unresponsive. Language started slowing down, then stopped. She stumbled more. Then, she needed a wheelchair; it was part of Moy's degenerative disorder. People would come to the McGowan–Chopra household and see a completely unresponsive teenager in a chair. No smile, no reaction to a comment or question, nothing. Everyone who saw Jo and Ravi with Moy Moy in this phase of her life remark on their behaviour.

'You'd think, "Oh my God, this severely disabled kid is dressed so nicely, she's sitting at the table for meals, being asked her opinions,"' remembers Shaila Faleiro. 'And there is no response from the child. None. It's just an awesome culture of the family.'[56] In so many households in India, disability is seen as a curse or an embarrassment to be hidden away from the external world. This full-blown involvement in all aspects of a family's life is jaw-dropping in contrast. Shaila, like other visitors over the years, was awestruck.

Yet, over time, Shaila recognized a deeper, subtler trait of Jo and Ravi as parents. 'Now when I see it, it is not a 'special' treatment,' she says. 'To them, Moy is our child just like Cathleen and Anand are. So, Cathleen is studious. She won a Fulbright scholarship. Anand is funny and entrepreneurial. And Moy, charming and adorable, has disabilities. The common thread is that all three are "our children."' That perspective and deeply held belief suffuses every action of theirs. Shaila describes Jo and Ravi's mindset: 'Yes, Moy Moy has physical and mental differences. So? She can still have fun, birthdays, be taken on trips.'[57] One small glimpse into the Jo–Moy relationship: Jo regularly read aloud to Moy, even when Moy stopped speaking and was facially unresponsive. When Moy was in her twenties, Jo realized that she was still reading out children's books, and switched. It was young-adult fiction then, and later, whatever Jo was reading herself.

It is that same fierce belief in the equality of children and how they should be treated that Jo took from her home with Moy Moy in it, to her organization. At Latika the children come first (always). They are treated with dignity and respect. Do 'normal' children without disabilities not love jokes, playing, colours and laughter? Why should any of that be held back from the Latika children? It is this single trait that turbo-charges everything – not limited to an individual or to one child, it is offered to *all* children. Yes, these children have disabilities ... so what?

Latika's office walls are lined with vibrant photographs of the children. One such beautifully framed photograph quotes Zen Buddhist teacher Shunryu Suzuki:

> 'Light up one corner – not the whole world, just make it clear where you are.'

3

Designing for the Most Vulnerable

A tall, lean woman strides on to the stage exuding confidence. Her short hair almost fully white, her glasses a dark purple. 'I have taken many leaps in my life,' she says to the TEDx audience in Kashipur, India. 'But first I want to tell you a little bit about myself.' And then, this white American in western clothes (a fluffy black and white sweater, and brown, knee-length boots), breaks into pristine, free-flowing Hindi, '*Kyo ki log mujhe dekh ke thoda (Jigyasa) hote hain*' ("People look at me and are curious"). '*Yeh kaun hai?*' ("Who is she?") '*Yahan kaisi pohanchi?*' ("How did she get here?") Then, beaming an extra-wide grin at the audience, she asks: '*Aur sabse bada ... aise acchhi Hindi kaise bolti hain?*' ("And most importantly... how does she speak such wonderful Hindi?")

Less than a minute into her talk, Jo Chopra McGowan has the audience riveted. Her energy is resoundingly palpable even through a grainy recording on YouTube.[58] She's at the TEDx event to tell her story as the founder of Latika.

'An estimated 1.3 billion people experience significant disability. This represents 16 per cent of the world's population, or one in six of us,' states a World Health Organization fact sheet.[59] Many are children who live with disabilities that range from moderate to severe.[60] How do you serve the most vulnerable? Latika tackles this question every single day.

'Parents who have kids with special needs tend to be angry or in denial initially,' says Ena Gaur, a special educator and former Latika Board member. 'The kid can be ignored. The parents are struggling, feeling guilty, or trying to justify why this happened to them.'[61] At Latika, the parents find a place where they are listened to; their child assessed by highly skilled professionals. Both child and parent can learn, slowly, with a lot of hard work, all that is needed to live a better, balanced life.

Latika's services start at birth and continue into adulthood. That, in itself, is noteworthy. In most Indian cities, as Ena points out, 'there is no place where you get all services under one roof – you have to run around from therapist to doctor, to counsellor, to play-group. You're skipping work, looking for childcare for your other child, and it's all so expensive.'[62] There is also a dearth of educators, physiotherapists, psychologists, paediatric doctors, occupational therapists and other skilled professionals who specialize in assisting children with disabilities. For example, India has fewer than ten paediatric doctors per 100,000 children, while Brazil has more than fifty and the United States has more than a hundred.[63] In India, the few experts available are mostly in the big cities, over-worked and severely stretched. In such a situation, especially if you aren't wealthy, Latika is a godsend.

Latika has had its share of teething trouble, obstacles and bumps. There have been wrong turns taken and opportunities missed. It is far from perfect and much remains to be done. Yet, taking all that into consideration, it is still a story filled with sparkle.

The first port of call for new, nervous parents is Gubbara, the assessment centre. They are welcomed and calmed by Sandeep Khanna, its quiet, gentle practitioner–manager. Autism, visual impairment, hearing issues, cerebral palsy, locomotor disabilities – his team has seen it all.

'"Will we be able to help?" is the question I ask every time. Talking and working with parents is very emotional,' says Sandeep.[64] A child new to Latika is asked to come in daily for a week. The first day is just observation. The Gubbara staff make notes: carefully watching the child play, rest, eat, or how a parent is feeding or toilet training. Observations cover everything from posture and daily activities, to academics. When the week is up, parents are given a comprehensive plan: an assessment and full report that contain diagnosis, suggestions of intervention through physical therapy and behavioural change at home, legal and governmental resources. The report is provided free of charge. A month later, Latika follows up, inviting the family back.

'At Latika you are appreciated for what you do, however big or small,' Sandeep says. 'That then makes you want to do more.' He is a physiotherapist with specialization in neurology, and has been with Latika since the early days; doing everything from changing curtains to painting rooms. Sandeep's daughter was born soon after he joined the organization. 'I would see her growing normally at home, then come to work and see slow progress among the children here,' he says. 'It helped me become a better therapist; to model what needed to be done rather than lecture the parents.'[65] To-date, Gubbara has assessed more than 5,500 children, monitored more than 400 high-risk babies in hospitals and provided outreach services to hundreds of children who live outside the city.[66] For each of them, Gubbara has charted out a more optimistic future.

After being assessed, if a child is less than six years old, the family comes to the Early Intervention Centre (EIC). The earlier a disability is diagnosed and support provided, the better a child does. EIC shows parents what is possible. Dr Linda Upadhyaya, who was at Latika from 2000-2015 was very influential in seeding the idea for the EIC. 'We were getting older kids and Linda said we should be doing babies,' remembers Jo.[67] It is important to build on what a child *can* do, rather than what she cannot. 'It is agreed by all educators and doctors that early intervention is *the* key factor for a child's physical, cognitive and emotional development,' says Paula Hughes, a special educator from England, 'so the EIC is a significant addition to Latika, a huge step forward.'[68]

Pooja Panwar, the Head of EIC, has, by her own admission, gone from, 'a shy, young girl to a confident woman,' in her twenty-three years at Latika. 'It is good for us to catch them early,' she says, echoing Paula's words. 'The entire team sits together: the therapist, the special educator, the counsellor and the parent.'[69] The child is assessed, a baseline created, a development plan with milestones chalked out. For example, if a young child has cerebral palsy, then the milestones include neck control, rolling over, the production of sounds and a social smile. (A social smile is when a baby makes the connection and responds to a familiar face like that of a parent. It is an intentional smile, as compared to a reflexive one.)

'The counsellor is a must,' emphasizes Pooja. 'She is the connection between the Latika team and parents. The parents are so traumatized when the baby is small and has just been diagnosed.' Latika mandates three sessions with the counsellor. 'The mother particularly, experiences so much – anxiety, blame from other family members, pressure from in-laws. She may have financial support from her husband but not physical support,' says Pooja.[70] The three sessions ensure that the parents, especially the mother, absorb details they might miss in a single session: the diagnosis, all the medical terms, the information on therapy sessions, what to expect in the child's growth, and so on. Latika's EIC works with about seventy-five children every year.[71]

For children between seven and fourteen, there is the Latika School. It caters to children with disabilities who are able to communicate and have higher cognition, and those whose disabilities might be more challenging and therefore need very high support.

Children in red and white uniforms tumble joyfully out of the Latika school vans and buses. UNESCO states that a majority of children with disabilities do not attend school.[72] In India, children with disabilities often live in the shadows, tucked away by families ashamed or embarrassed by their differences. 'Other schools say we don't have a special needs teacher. Or we can't take responsibility for your child,' says Neelam Rawat, whose son, Ayush, has Down syndrome. 'Ayush's mind will be like a five-year-old,' she says, 'so, he cannot be in the same class as his age group. In a younger class, the other parents worry that your older, bigger child will hit their children.'[73]

At the Latika school, these children, mistreated and ignored elsewhere, are front and centre, master of all that they survey. Their disabilities run the gamut: cerebral palsy and Down syndrome, developmental delays, learning difficulties that affect cognitive development, speech and language and gross and fine motor-skills, and the autistic spectrum. What radiates, though, is pure joy. Their self-confidence is palpable as they greet each other, walk in through the door with different gaits, or roll in on wheelchairs and show, through smiles, waves, pats on the arm, pleasure at being at *their* school.

Warmly welcomed by their teachers, they sing a prayer and the national anthem. Anne Bruce, a Scottish speech therapist from the UK's National Health System, who volunteered at Latika for almost a decade, says, 'The pleasure that the staff have in the children, the level of commitment even for the most difficult of children, and the amount of love they have – and "love" is a hard word for a Scottish person to say – is remarkable.' She points out that 'in Europe we are always told to be "professional," which means not being involved. They'd be shocked at Latika – the love, the involvement.'[74]

The school has two sessions, one from 9 a.m. to 12 noon, where the same children come every day, and one from 1 p.m. to 3 p.m., for parents who live far away and might be able to bring their children only once or twice a week. When Manju Subedi first took on the responsibility, there were twelve children. Now, there are 156 children from the age of six to fourteen.[75]

Activity-based learning is the basis of all teaching strategies at the school. Children are carefully assessed and educational plans drawn up with short- and long-term goals. They sit in groups around circular tables. Doing so develops social skills. All those at a table are, by and large, working on similar tasks, playing games, sharing space and paper, pencils, crayons.

For mathematics, a class could start with the teacher asking how many are at the table. It would be followed by: 'So, how many glasses of water are needed?' A progression would be to provide fewer glasses of water than children, and ask: 'How many *more* glasses are needed?' Functional literacy is strengthened using, for example, the days of the week (in Hindi) with the day displayed on a board. "What day will it be tomorrow?' 'What day was it yesterday?'

A simple, popular outdoor game is hopscotch. Paula Hughes points out, 'Playing hopscotch focuses largely on developing gross motor-skills, adapted to the level of the individual player. Some children are learning to hop, some [are] jumping, others are simply learning to balance as they stand in one square and toss the marker to the next square. In addition,' she adds, 'there's the social skill of taking turns and number recognition and sequences. But also, the children are just having fun.'[76]

A red circle *bindi*, a yellow square play-mat, wet sand and dry sand to play in, a rectangular door; shapes, colours, sizes and textures are learned by looking around. 'Singing and dancing are everyday activities,' says Paula, 'along with free-drawing and painting. These activities not only help language and motor skills but are essential for emotional development.'[77]

Not all activities are in groups. If a child is hitting others or throwing objects, becoming unmanageable, he is gently withdrawn from the group. Trained volunteers keep him company, sitting, walking, talking, until he calms down. This could take anywhere from a few minutes to an hour.

'The lecture method doesn't work,' says Ena Gaur describing the curriculum. 'You have to change academic content, teaching methods, help them respect themselves. A lot of emotional work is done.' There is plenty of paperwork for the staff – lesson planning, assessment of the skill level of each child (a ten-year-old might be reading or behaving at the level of a five-year-old), documentation, and so on. The special education teachers at Latika learn to do all this, but also to celebrate the small victories. 'The child who used to hide in the bathroom during reading class is now sitting in a corner, quietly,' says Ena. 'That is progress.'[78]

'He has learnt to wear his own clothes, eat, brush his teeth and hair and bathe himself,' says Neelam Rawat about her eleven-year-old. Friendship is a powerful thing, especially for those who do not have easy access to it. 'He loves the Latika school; he has made friends and enemies too in class. They hug, they fight,' Neelam says. Then with a laugh that lights up her beautiful, serious face she adds, 'In the holidays they want to chat on the phone, even though neither can talk!'[79]

'It is not all school-centred,' says Manju Subedi, the bubbly, effervescent Head of the Latika School, about the learning. 'We do a lot of trips to the world outside: how does a petrol pump work? The children learn, for example: how far can you go on a bicycle? A motorcycle? A train? A plane? We have taken them to the railway station, and are hoping to visit the airport.' Preparation is key. 'For the petrol-pump visit, they role-played with the Latika vans and drivers, using pipes as demonstration.' Manju and her team cannot emphasize enough how *much* these school trips help a child's development. 'Children learn attention, waiting [being patient], observing – so much,' she says. 'Of course, we have to be careful that no one gets hurt, but it is so valuable.'[80]

'We don't see men cry,' says Manju. The school children had recently visited a petrol pump. A father came to Manju broke down in tears and said, 'I was filling my motorcycle, my son was with me. He suddenly said, 'petrol.' I have never heard him say that before. And it was because of you; he learnt it in *this* school.'[81]

One of the most heart-warming activities involved the post office. 'Step by step we wrote a letter in class,' says Manju. 'Then we all went to the post office and posted the letters to their homes. Without telling the parents!' It was an incredible, joyful surprise for the families. 'It didn't matter whether there was something written, or a drawing, a thumb impression or just a scribble,' says Manju, 'they got mail from their child!'[82]

Sometimes, interventions do not have to be early, they have to be timely. Take menstruation, for instance. How do you explain menstruation to a child with special needs? What it implies? What has to be done in private rather than in front of family members and neighbours?

Latika has a special menstruation class for girls who are nine or ten years old. The teacher has a doll, panties, a sanitary pad, newspaper, a dustbin, a wash basin, soap and a towel. She uses ink to depict menstrual blood. Then, she slowly and repeatedly shows the girls how to stick a clean sanitary pad to the panty, how to remove a used one, to wrap it in newspaper, discard it, dispose of it, wash hands with soap, and wipe on the towel. The teacher instructs them to prep the panties two days before their periods – so when the time comes there is no stress. The girls come up to the table, and one by one try it. While the girls are learning this, their mothers sit at the back of the room, observant but, on request, silent. 'They see that the child is doing it so well in class. We tell the mothers to observe. Notice their own child,' remarks Manju Subedi.[83] The mother realizes that her child can do this on her own, perhaps with a little assistance.

Despite all the effort, it isn't always a clear trajectory of 'demonstrate in school and all goes well at home.' Manju describes a desperate call her team got recently. A mother found that her daughter, who has cerebral palsy, had not changed her sanitary napkin in two days. She was screaming and lashing out when her mother tried to get her to change. 'The mother said it was a battle... Neighbours began to ask what the screaming was about. She was desperate. I spoke to our team, the counsellor, teachers and others,' says Manju.

For the next three days, the Latika team asked the mother and daughter to come in. They used the school bathroom, switched on the geyser for hot water, and taught the young girl how to do things, how to keep herself clean. 'First, we did hands-on,' she says, 'then we stood back and saw how the child does it on the mother's saying so.'[84] Thus, with a lot of love and care, girls with disabilities are helped to transition into menstruation and all that it involves.

The children under Manju's care are 'the higher cognitive children, who communicate, have fewer behavioural issues and are easier to handle. The children who come to us are more challenging,' says Sunita Singh about her team, at the Latika School. 'For example, a child cannot express himself. He cannot say, 'I am thirsty, give me water.' So, he hits himself or throws things.'[85]

The team works with the child and parents to use simple words, or if he does not have language, to use other forms like facial expressions or gestures to indicate thirst. 'We show parents that these are not behavioural issues, it is a way of communicating, so we need to change to a different way of communication.'[86]

'The parents come highly anxious,' says Sunita. 'Our main work is parents' empowerment and managing their expectations for their children.' Much of the work involves behaviour, communication, speech and language therapy. The team strives to address the roots of behaviour. 'Behavioural issues need to be minimized, because they become barriers to further learning and growth; especially in highly functioning kids with autism,' Sunita points out.[87] There are currently eighty-one children with Sunita and her team.[88]

It isn't enough to identify the issues, chalk up a plan for the child, do the therapy at Latika and tell the parents what to do at home. Often, the mother has no support from her family, she is already over-burdened, and under a lot of stress from her husband or in-laws. 'We have to shore up support at home,' says Sunita. 'We can't just hand out extra tasks for her to do.' Members of her team spend a lot of time counselling the parents, especially the mother. They provide techniques and strategies that she can experiment with. 'We demonstrate at Latika. We tell them, you can call us, we can do home visits.' For children with severe challenges, the team has learnt that much of the work *has to* happen outside Latika. 'If all is only done at Latika, then it is of no use,' says Sunita. 'We have to see it in the community, in his school, in his home. Just being good here is not enough.'[89]

Across the main road from Latika, you enter a gate and turn right. A physical separation that is psychological as well – this is Latika's Centre for Vocational Training (CVT).

At fourteen, children graduate from the Latika School. On their way to young adulthood, their needs, physicality, and with an eye to the future, their skills, call for a different format. The enthusiasm that Prem Singh, the Head of CVT, exudes, is like a river in flood: you get completely swept up. In under an hour, you are told about the centre, shown videos, informed of experiments in progress, introduced to participants, parents...the entire panorama. A highly trained physiotherapist, Prem joined Latika in 2008, intending to leave in a year, after gaining some experience. 'I wasn't planning to stay, but that's destiny,' he says.[90]

At CVT there are seventy-six young people between the ages of fourteen and twenty-one who are trained, as much as possible, for an occupation and to help at home. Young adults with disabilities learn about everything from stitching, housekeeping, gardening and shop-keeping to office support and computer skills.[91] The hope is that love, care and practical training will help them find meaningful jobs and some degree of independence. Prem divides the working world into three categories, based on skills and abilities: 'There is sheltered employment that needs constant supervision, like making candles. There is supervised employment, like being an assistant in a shop. And finally, there is open employment; what most adults without disabilities, like you and me, do.'[92] At CVT, the focus is on training for some form of supervised employment.

Teaching and training, though challenging, is the easier part; much harder is the effort needed to change society. 'There is so much resistance,' says

Prem. 'In all these years, no local business has come to us offering a job. We have to do a market survey. See what is available, persuade the bakery or the small office to take our children.'[93]

Prem is talking about a problem that extends far beyond Dehradun. Unemployment among the disabled can be as high as 80 per cent, says the International Labour Organization. In India, which has millions with disabilities, only around 100,000 have found employment outside the government sector (which reserves some jobs for the disabled).[94] It is harder for Latika because its children have multiple disabilities. 'They would be easier to place if he or she was only hearing impaired or blind,' Prem says. Sometimes, difficulties arise because employers are simply unprepared for candour. 'Our children, especially those with Down syndrome, are very frank. They are not able to mask their opinions or feelings,' Prem says, with a grin. The employer is often aghast at such raw honesty. 'So, we now have a session that teaches the children that masking or being polite is not telling lies. It is how they have to navigate the working world.'[95]

Mahindar Singh Kumar, is a tall, burly man of few words. Yet, while talking about his son, Maneshwar, he is movingly eloquent. His family came to Latika after trying eight doctors. His son is hyperactive, has convulsions and a severe mental disability. As his son grew, Mahindar realized it was too much for his wife to manage. So, he sought early retirement from the Indian Army. At fourteen, his son has recently transitioned from the Latika school to CVT. 'My son couldn't sit. Latika taught him over one year how to sit,' says Mahindar. 'His mind had no attention – now he has some focus. Here they look at the person, not the wealth or the status. They help. There is no exploitation.'[96]

Mahindar's made peace with his son not being 'normal' and all that it entails. He and his wife travel a long three-hour round trip every day to Latika, but they do it with appreciation. 'We might clean our son's snot or wipe the spit off his face, but would you do it for other children?' he asks. 'Here, I have seen them do it with such love. And with no hesitation.'[97]

After some silence, Mahindar says, 'In this life that we have, you have to be positive. Otherwise, it is full of sorrow. We worship our gods in the form of stone statues, yet we bathe, feed and clean the statues.' Choking up, he adds, 'It is like that with our son – there are no outward signs from him, but we do it with love. This is all we have to do, look after him.'[98]

To belong, to have someone to laugh with, to just hang out together. All this is much harder for a child with special needs, especially as she grows into a young adult. 'Children with neurodevelopmental disabilities are often excluded and experience more loneliness than their typically developing peers,' report John-Paul Collet and his colleagues at the University of British Columbia, adding that such loneliness was associated with 'negative consequences on mental health, behaviour, and psychosocial or emotional development, with a likely long-term impact.'[99]

Jo and her colleagues spotted this loneliness. In response, they did something simple but noteworthy: they started a club. If you are over twenty-one, you can join. About forty-five people have enrolled and typically ten or fifteen come for the twice-a-week gathering. 'It becomes very hard to keep friends, especially with intellectual disabilities,' says Prem, echoing all the academic research done on the subject. The club has music, dancing and games. It uses the vocational centre's lounge, with its comfortable sofas and television. A teacher and her assistant are there to facilitate the games, but it is all much more informal than the school. Next to the lounge is a large kitchen. Here club members learn how to cook and serve. A young man with Down syndrome comes around taking orders. He's wearing a chequered apron and holding a large sheet of paper – the menu in pictures. Today's offering is tea, soup and *poha*; twenty rupees each. He slowly approaches every individual in the building asking, 'Didi, Bhaiya, what will you order?' Every person orders at least one dish; with such a beaming smile in return, how could you refuse?

'Alone, you get stared at,' remarks Prem, 'but in a group, you get strength.' The club members go on hikes, they go to restaurants, they dance in open fields. 'Outings are important – they learn new things. Simultaneously, the outside world learns about disability,' Prem says.[100]

Hang around Latika one evening and you will see a lot of activity and laughter in the playground. Latika's inclusive after-school programme is for those between the ages of three and fifteen. It has around seventy children with and without disabilities.[101] This is the origin of Latika, which started as a play group for Jo's three children.

The children have fun, sing, dance, do pottery, play ball, and generally have a good time without constant adult intervention. Youngsters like Kashvi, a thirteen-year-old girl who has Down syndrome, have been coming for years. They pretty much run the place. According to her mother, Kusum, she adores the evening play. 'Come 4 p.m. she says, "Mamma let's go, let's go,"' says Kusum.[102]

Kusum draws out the interconnection of the Latika services. Therapy done at school during the day shows up in better behaviour on the playground in the evening. 'Kashvi used to spit a lot, especially when people asked her to do things she didn't want to do,' recalls Kusum. 'We worked with all the Latika teachers for three years.' Now, her mother says, 'She is so social, everyone knows her.'[103]

'In a mall or a family function, parents are always so conscious about their child being stared at,' says Ena Gaur. 'At the after-school programme, the first thing that strikes you is that nobody is staring. Your child can be who they are. It puts a young parent, who may be doubting their parenting skills, at ease.'[104] When you look at the parents' faces as they watch their children playing, laughing, you see relief and a quiet appreciation. Your child is accepted; she's scampering around with nobody judging what she looks like or what she isn't capable of.

Managing all these vibrant services and centres, including providing vital legal, child protection, advocacy, evaluation and monitoring services, is Latika's Resource Centre.

Providing much-needed end-to-end services for children with disabilities was a dream come true. Not all of Jo's dreams for Latika were met immediately. Sometimes, it took years for an idea to bear fruit. 'Plant trees under whose shade you do not expect to sit,' is a quote one often hears. At Latika, there is an entire grove of such trees.

4

Seeds That Blossom Later

An oak tree can live for nine centuries. An entire world of animals, birds and fungi is sheltered by this one magnificent tree. The oak, it turns out, is not great at self-propagation. When it drops its acorns (after twenty years of growing), they either rot under the shade of the parent tree or are hoovered up as a delicious snack by deer and squirrels. To propagate, what the oak needs is the jay. Choosing the best ones, carrying six at a time in its beak, the bird hides the acorns for when food is scarce. Each acorn is hammered deep into the open ground to prevent mice from eating it, with a thorny bush nearby as a visual reminder. When other food is easily available, the bird doesn't harvest its stock. Even when it does, all that has been hidden is not gathered. Thus does the oak perpetuate itself.[105]

Latika is the oak with its wide reach and evolving, nourishing eco-system. And it has many jays. Over the decades, remarkable people have come through its doors, staying for varying lengths of time. India has a history of foreigners contributing to the country's development. They have either settled here, or visited long enough to make an impact. Samuel Stokes, an American, was arrested for his role in India's freedom movement. He introduced apple cultivation in the state of Himachal Pradesh. Laurie Baker, a British architect, settled in Kerala and was a pioneer in sustainable architecture with local materials. The list is long and varied. Similarly, at Latika, international volunteers have played a big role in the organization's growth. Their ideas and dreams, however, have taken time to fructify.

Nicola Tansley was one of Latika's jays. An educational psychologist who ran a special school in England, she spent many months in the early 2000s, in Dharamshala, working with Tibetan refugee children. That work brought her to a Tibetan school in Dehradun, which in turn led to meeting Jo. Nicola taught the Latika staff the value of mentorship: How do you supervise in a reflective manner? In a directive manner? She emphasized documentation and planning: How to read the past history of a child, take notes, think through the plan for the future. How do you think critically? 'She did it with our counsellors and psychologists,' recalls Jo. 'Nobody in the Indian system is taught that at all. *Why* are you doing what you are doing? What can change? *How* do we plan? We could see the staff blossom right in front of our eyes.'[106]

While she was involved in mentoring and many creative activities like creating a library for the children, Nicola's passion was children's rights.[107] She was clear that Latika needed a child-protection policy that was child-centric and would click into place no matter the situation. A teacher helps a child pin his drawing to the cork-board; he pricks his finger by mistake. It is noticed a few days later by his mother and the incident snowballs into accusations and questions. A voluble, friendly girl goes disquietingly silent in school. However small the incident – or however grave – Latika needed clearly defined steps for what happens next.

Too often, the very adults who are in charge of a child's well-being – teachers, parents, doctors, nurses, police – find it hard to believe and easy to belittle an incident, because the alternative is to confront an unpleasant truth, shatter existing relationships, and bring ugliness into bright sunshine.

A robust child-protection policy takes on urgency if the children involved have disabilities. A non-verbal child may know something bad has happened but cannot put it into words; a teacher may see repeated bruises on a young boy with autism but does not know whether to bring up the issue with his parents, as it may be the parents hitting the boy. What happens if the parents close rank, turn around and accuse the teacher?

Like many projects that have the best of intentions, not much head-way was made. Daily work was overwhelming; it was difficult to make time for policies that are not deployed every day. Nicola embedded the seeds of child-protection at Latika. And then, she left. What was needed was an on-the-ground champion.

Latika has many bright personalities; people who charge the very air they walk through. Sumita Nanda is one of the quiet ones. Trim and erect, she wears kurtas in pastel colours, embroidered with delicate flowers. As Chief Operations Officer (COO), she is fluent in English, but quickly admits that Hindi is her language of comfort. She has risen through the ranks at Latika, from receptionist to COO. Her methodical nature sometimes makes it hard to detect the spark that motivates her.

Sumita's serene face becomes animated when she talks about two things: her debt to Jo (for giving her a chance and mentoring her at Latika), and child protection. 'I offered to take up the work that Nicola started years ago, so I became the Child Protection Officer,' she says.[108] With help from Nicola and Ajay Sharma, Sumita studied other organizations' policies, learnt what it meant to be a Protection Officer, and worked on how the policy should work at Latika. 'We had the policy in place, but systems and processes had to be strengthened. There was a gap between when something happened and when the information came to us,' Sumita says.[109]

Her first case came a few weeks after she took responsibility for child protection. In conversation with a female teacher, a girl at the Latika school said a male staff member had touched her chest. A month had gone by since the incident occurred. 'There was so much tension. Jo was not in town,' recalls Sumita. 'But we had a clear process. Even if the person accused denies it, which he did, he is suspended while the case is investigated.' After due diligence, the man was asked to leave.

The case showed Sumita a number of gaps between having a robust policy on paper and one in action. 'Why did it take so long? Why was the girl alone with the male teacher in the room? It turned out that the (female) helper had taken another child to the bathroom. We had to fix all that,' Sumita says.[110]

Children may find it difficult to put experiences into words. They may be unwilling or unable to name those who harm them. A recent study of children with disabilities and child protection services notes that 'Children with intellectual disabilities (ID) are more vulnerable to maltreatment than children without ID. ...Professionals play a preponderant role in reporting situations of maltreatment for children with ID and need additional training to properly respond.'[111] Sumita has incorporated child protection into every part of Latika: teaching, training, recruitment, evaluations. Seasoned staffers, new recruits, interns – all get to learn it, because child protection is not just Sumita's job, it is *everyone's* job.

Sumita and her team have translated policy guidelines into tools and processes. For non-verbal children, Latika has drawings of the human body to which a child can point. For all children, Latika has psychologists who can gently gather information. Along with training, all staff members sign a legal agreement on child protection and promise to report any incident immediately to the head of their centre or to the Child Protection Officer. 'Immediately means,' clarifies Sumita, 'that they will stop everything else and go directly, without even a five-minute delay.'[112]

The body map helps not just the children – Latika employees use it to report in detail: How big was the bruise? Was it on the elbow or the shoulder? Is there a pattern? They do not have to rely on memory alone. Writing also puts on paper what might otherwise vanish in the flurry of daily activity. A robust policy on child protection reassures parents, employees and funders that Latika is a safe place for children with disabilities. It is a lot of work, but anything less is not good enough.

The system isn't perfect. An evaluation in 2019 noted that 'A process of making learning about child protection easily accessible is already underway' and recommended that Latika pay attention to 'learning from any incident.'[113]

'I think we now understand the complexity and the challenge of what we are trying to do,' states Jo. 'Every situation we've dealt with so far has been confusing and ambiguous. We know someone hurt a child, but we aren't sure who. Or we do know who, but it's a family member and the family closes rank. Once we were sure there was something bad going on, but there was no hard evidence.'[114] Sumita recognizes the challenge of bringing about change, of preventing complacency. 'We are sharing the cases with our colleagues: what happened; what should have been done. They need to sit down and write incidents and report *immediately*.'

For the child? Her answer is unequivocal: 'We never question. We *always* believe the child.'[115]

The sooner a disability is diagnosed, the better the chance for parents to adapt and learn to build a fulfilling life. Sebastian Gruschke, a doctor from the Netherlands, was instrumental in honing Latika's early intervention model over almost a decade.

If you want to help the poor, nothing beats working with the government. Coca-Cola reaches 520 million customers in Latin America and 2 billion customers in Africa, the Middle East and Europe. In every one of those regions, the government reaches more people.

In healthcare, affordability and accessibility are challenges. The International Finance Corporation (IFC) works across the globe to combine private-sector companies (which run hospitals or provide insurance or diagnostic services), with government systems. The idea is that these public-private partnerships will improve the quality and efficiency of healthcare services provided to millions of poor individuals. In Mexico, for instance, in an IFC project, a hospitals partnership with the government aimed to cover one million people being served. Similarly, in Meghalaya, India, an IFC project brought health insurance coverage to three million people who were just above the poverty-line, and thus not able to access existing government insurance available to the poor.[116]

Such partnerships, however, are not smooth sailing. It is difficult, with different assessments of risk on each side, to make the approaches mesh smoothly. Roles between partners may not be clearly defined. There may be a lack of trust between the two sides.[117] Paperwork seems to metastasize. Teams struggling to provide affordable services to the poor sometimes find that there is not much room to maneuver or be creative.

Like a pop-up restaurant with all the related pizzazz, Latika broke multiple barriers by starting an assessment, early intervention and resource centre, Gubbara, right *within* a public hospital. The partnership was brokered by an honest, intellectually curious and politically sharp government official named Keshav Desiraju, who went on to become the Health Secretary, Government of India. Desiraju was intrigued by Jo's laying out the case that by intervening and investing early in a child's development you can mitigate or even prevent disability, saving the government plenty of money in disability services in the future.

He visited Latika and became a staunch supporter of the organization. 'Often it is difficult to find people in the health ministry who see the importance of this kind of work,' says Sebastian. 'It was a very nice time – to see the cooperation between the government and Latika. The combination of the Latika therapists and the Doon Hospital doctors was excellent. Everything in one place – that was very good!'[118]

Sebastian worked as a doctor and coordinator of all resources available to parents. Fluent in Hindi, he would communicate parents' questions to the doctors in the government hospital, look at the medical papers of the child, see what medical investigations were done, check if anything further was needed. 'You need someone to look at the whole domain of the functioning of the child,' he says. 'Latika has all the therapists, but each did [only] their part. Someone needs to get an overall picture – cognitive, social, physical functioning, food, to work on the whole picture, and make a plan of what is to be done.'[119]

Working right inside Doon Hospital, the city's biggest public hospital, was a boon not only for Latika but also for the government doctors. 'For them Latika is very helpful,' points out Sebastian, 'because every day there are about 80 to 100 children waiting to see the doctor. Of these, at least three or four would have cerebral palsy or another disability. It was very nice for them to be able to send the kids to us. They didn't have the time or knowledge. Latika had more specialized knowledge of what to do and what could not be done.'[120]

Edmund Cluett and Angie Toppan only came to Latika for a year, but left iridescent changes. Edmund taught Jo photography, a skill that makes Latika's work come alive on the internet, in presentations, annual reports and Latika's much-anticipated calendars, which are filled with striking photographs and inspiring quotes. Jo's photographs portray something that is rarely captured in the world of disability: pure joy.

Jo, in turn, mentored Manik, now the chief photographer at Latika. 'Edmund taught me pretty much all I know about taking pictures,' Jo recalled later. 'Apertures, f-stops, depth of field, low light, composition and how to hold a camera properly were all part of the lessons, but the most essential thing I learned was how to *look* at what I am photographing. "What are you taking a picture of?" he would ask me over and over again. "What are you trying to say?"'[121]

Paula Hughes had no burning desire to come to India. There was no interest in yoga, no wish to spot a flame-striped tiger. 'I was wondering what on Earth was I doing so far from my family in such a chaotic, hot, noisy place,' she says. 'During the longest train journey I had ever taken (one I later realized was actually nothing in terms of journeys in India), I convinced myself that I would forget everything I had ever learned about education and I would be found wanting. Well, never mind, perhaps they'd be disappointed and send me home. Problem solved!'[122]

Having dropped out of college to raise her family, Paula worked as a teaching assistant in a school for children with moderate learning difficulties. When she was in her forties, her children left for college and her husband died. Instead of collapsing, she poured that emptiness into training as a special education teacher. She came to Latika in 1995 through a British organization called Volunteers for Services Overseas (VSO). It was a two-year contract; Paula stayed for twelve.

'I expected the school would be established; that I would train the teachers to work using [an] activity-based approach to their existing curriculum,' Paula says.[123] She was shocked to find Latika in its early days.

Paula thus became the de-facto leader of a start-up. 'Paula never stopped amazing us,' wrote Jo. '[Watching her transform into a leader] made us realize that the only limits on a person's potential are the arbitrary ones we ourselves impose. People are capable of almost anything. It was a revelation.'[124] Ravi says of Paula, 'She never learnt even a smattering of Hindi and yet she could communicate. For example, there was a little girl who would scream her head off. Paula would just put her in her lap and put her arms around her. By doing things her way, she taught a lot to the Latika staff.'[125]

In the early years, everyone did everything. If the cleaner did not come, Paula would scrub the toilets. If the driver was on leave, Jo leapt into the van for the pick-up run around the city. 'I felt a little socially inept as Jo and her Indian friends clearly had a high social status. Perhaps as a Brit I was too conscious of things like class,' Paula remarks. 'I was fascinated to hear how they switched from Hindi to English mid-sentence.' When things went wrong at Latika, and they often did, Paula would cheerfully remark, 'Never mind! Worse things happen at sea!'[126]

The Latika school for children with disabilities, grew under Paula's tender care. In her twelve years, Paula went much beyond special education training and administrative detail. She planted four particular seeds of organizational and cultural change at Latika.

Paying attention

Helping children with special needs can be extremely frustrating. There is a stop-start aspect to the work that teachers in mainstream schools rarely encounter. Book learning comes much later, after areas like social skills, emotional development and behavioural learning; capabilities that exams seldom capture. Paula, as a special educator, taught the young Latika school teachers and assistants *how* to pay attention, how to see.

In a beautiful essay from 2011, Paula celebrates milestones that might be invisible to an outsider: 'An improvement in the attention span of one child – she could now complete a puzzle without demanding adult attention. An increase in confidence in another child ... standing in line, for ten seconds only, but in line. Oh wow!'[127]

In mainstream schools, improvement is measured by exam results. At Latika, progress is more finely shaded, built slowly and not always in a progressive trajectory. 'Mayank's ten seconds achievement had developed one or two seconds at a time,' Paula writes, 'increasing not daily but slowly over the months and interspersed with pauses and occasional backward steps, the slow rate of growth almost unnoticeable.'[128] Paula taught the Latika staff that while it can sometimes seem that there is no growth, even perhaps a decline in skill development, that is rarely the case. All one has to do is slow down, observe closely, see the small, often, minuscule changes – *that* is where you find learning and encouragement.

Play matters greatly

The second seed planted by Paula is now a tenet of the Latika-way of doing things. Play matters to all children but especially children with disabilities. 'They need it,' she emphasizes. 'We made sure Latika was a fun, playful place, even when we were doing serious work. It was so important that the place not be miserable, but cheerful, with bright colours,' she recalls.[129] Play that is not squashed into a tight schedule, but is an active component of how teaching takes place; how skills are introduced and honed; how even teachers themselves learn – all these became a part of Latika's DNA.

Researchers studying children with autism spectrum disorders have proposed that 'imitation, joint attention, and play are pivotal abilities in early development, and that intervention for young children with autism should incorporate these abilities as treatment goals.' They emphasize play. 'By exploring and manipulating objects, [children] learn to think flexibly and creatively, which benefits their problem-solving abilities. Young children ... perfect their newly acquired language abilities in play ... Apart from this cognitive and emotional function, play also has a social function when children play together.'[130]

Children want to learn

Paula's third contribution was simple yet profound: children *want* to learn. It does not matter whether they have a disability or what that disability is. Children are curious, thinking beings desirous of learning.

Paula put in the processes needed to encourage learning, to answer the question: if the children want to learn, what should the teacher do? The teacher has to learn how to work with that curiosity, that desire, and become a facilitator of the process of learning.

Respect for all

The most remarkable seed of Paula's legacy, though, has nothing to do with disability. In an Indian context, it is nothing short of radical.

'Paula taught us to be amazed by the ordinary people around us,' Jo recalls years later. '[People] who... are taken for granted as background furnishing.'[131] These are drivers, cleaners, plumbers, gardeners, cooks and the ubiquitous 'office boy' who keep homes and offices functioning. 'The thought of people as servants was very strange to me,' says Paula. Being British, she was very conscious of class and saw it everywhere in India. 'The term 'servant' really got to me. That attitude really upset me.'[132] Satpal, for example, worked at Latika, cleaning the place, making everyone tea numerous times a day, running errands. 'I really tried to make sure people saw him as one of us,' says Paula. 'That kind of thing is important to me. For people [in India] it's just a part of their lives, but I wanted to make sure that he is treated with the *same* respect.'[133]

How do you change deeply embedded cultural prejudices? Organizations have hierarchies – spend some time in a hospital and you may see a sharp divide between doctors and nurses, even though on a range of issues, it may be the nurses who have more contact with the patients, and thus, more experience. Journalist Charles Duhigg writes about the Rhode Island Hospital in the United States, where the surgeons ruled as such tyrants that the nurses had a secret colour-code for when they put doctors' names on the white-board. 'Blue meant "nice," red meant "jerk" and black meant "whatever you do, don't contradict them or they will take your head off."'[134]

The nurses were constantly correcting the doctors' mistakes, double-checking and re-writing orders so that patients received the correct doses of medicines or were operated on accurately. Toxic patterns developed in employee behaviour. 'It felt like working in a war zone ... everything was out of control,' a nurse said.[135] It took multiple patient deaths, fines from the government and detailed tracking by the media for the hospital to come to its senses. An overhaul of systems, processes and opening of conversations was needed for the culture to change.

Cultures are not always toxic, but hierarchies can manifest in multiple ways, sometimes visual. Companies have uniforms for factory workers but not the management, or different dining rooms depending on whether you are a 'blue-collar' worker or a 'white-collar' manager.[136]

There is a famous story in the automobile world of Toyota taking over General Motors' worst factory in the United States. The workers were so discontented that they would show up drunk, put empty bottles in the doors so that the new car would rattle when driven and much worse. Toyota used its famous Toyota Production System to transform the same factory, employing the *same* workers. It was a management and cultural revolution. John Shook, who witnessed this transformation, wrote: 'What my experience taught me that was so powerful was that the way to change culture is not to first change how people think, but instead to start by changing how people behave – what they do.'[137]

Over the years, Paula established a strong, inclusive culture by changing hierarchical behaviour. She brought into Latika a respect for all, especially the 'little' people – whether it is the security guard at the gate, the small donor or a young special-education assistant struggling with English. Just like nurses in a hospital, or engaged workers on the factory floor, she showed the Latika management how employees who might otherwise be ignored in decision-making, have enormous insight and capacity for improving the organization based on their observations on the ground.

Years after her departure, her achievement manifests itself in many ways: the language of work and office is Hindi (not English, which divides); everyone is called Didi or Bhaiya; the Resource Centre staff (the management) seek and respect inputs from assistants and drivers; the bathrooms and dining table are shared by all; even the person who opens the gate at Latika demonstrates a quiet dignity of the job. Ravi adds to the examples of an absence of hierarchy, 'at Latika, any person going in a car must sit in the passenger seat next to the driver. Not at the back, like a "fancy *sahib*".'[138]

Sandeep Khanna, became head of Gubbara, the assessment centre, many years after Paula's departure. He remembers how, in all his education and previous work experience, 'I was used to "Ma'am" and "Sir". It created a big barrier.' As he started calling others Bhaiya or Didi, Sandeep sensed a shift in himself and the parents he worked with. 'They immediately started telling me more things, chatting more,' he says. 'How I acted, changed.'[139]

Much of this cultural influence can be traced back to Paula's quiet spirit and how it has seeped into the organization. Jo writes, 'Paula taught us to see everyone [regardless of social status] as the treasures they are and that knowledge and belief became the backbone of Latika.'[140]

5

What's with the Name?

Is Jo's real name Latika? Until 2023, Latika, used to be the Latika Roy Memorial Foundation, a mouthful of a name. People assume that Jo McGowan, the founder, is actually Latika. Or that Latika was Jo's grandmother. Or Ravi's mother. None of it is true. Latika Roy was a pioneering woman of the twentieth century. Born at a time when boys were sent to school but girls kept home in purdah, she had only one searing question for her prospective grooms, 'When we marry, will you let me study?'[141]

Mrs Roy's sharp mind led her not just to study but to absorb all that was new and revolutionary in education. During the second world war, Maria Montessori, the famous Italian educator whose pedagogy bears her name, was held in internment in India. Mrs Roy heard of this, bundled her two-year-old son up, and took a train journey of more than 2,800 kilometres from Dehradun in the north to the southern hill-station of Kodaikanal, to learn from Dr Montessori. Upon her return Mrs Roy started teaching. She couldn't afford to rent a building, so she started in a shed. Children of Indian Army officers, of staff at the Forest Research Institute, children from other neighbourhoods, all enrolled. Her school still exists. It runs from kindergarten to twelfth grade, shaping more than 600 students every year.

In the last two decades of her life, Mrs Roy was bed-ridden, paralyzed by a series of strokes. 'Before she died, my mother kept saying it would be nice to have something with her name on it,' says Anubrotto Kumar Roy, her son, known to all as Dunu. That wish resulted in Dunu's father donating the money Jo needed to start an organization for children with disabilities. 'I remember eighty-five-year-old Mr Roy coming and telling me, "Let's do something for children in the memory of my wife,"' says Ravi. Ravi had fond memories, from his own childhood in Mumbai, of a local play centre: 'It had a lawn with games, a library, toys. I would go every evening, didn't miss a single day. It's my most cherished memory.'[142] Dunu says, 'My father guided Jo and the organization a lot in the early years. He would visit Latika every day, sit in a corner of the verandah, in his favourite chair and the kids would come, play and chat with him.'[143]

Thus did the organization come to be called Latika. There's poetic logic to the name as well: Latika is a version of Latha or *bel* in Hindi, a vine. A plant that needs support to grow and flower beautifully; much like the supportive guidance the organization provides to so many families and children with disabilities.

6

A Girl from Fall River, A Boy from Charni Road

Most American parents take their children to baseball games. The McGowans took theirs to protests. 'My parents would take us to demonstrations. We'd paint signs to carry. We did boycotts all the time,' says Jo of her childhood. 'We'd picket grocery stores for non-unionization. I raised money in tin cans for cerebral palsy.'[144]

It is the summer of 1976. The United States is roiling. The decade before has been tumultuous, with the civil rights movement and the hippie, counter-culture movement, all spilling messily into the 1970s. Millions are demanding rights: African-Americans, Native Americans, women, environmentalists. John Lennon has left the Beatles. His first solo single, 'Give

Peace a Chance,' is sung by half a million people protesting the Vietnam War.[145] President Richard Nixon, engulfed by the Watergate scandal, becomes the only US president to resign from office.

Halfway across the globe, India is in turmoil too. Its prime minister, Indira Gandhi, in an unprecedented grab for power, seeing internal threats from a vast people's movement, and externally from neighbouring countries, has suspended a democratically elected government and declared a national state of emergency. The future of democracy is in peril. Activists, journalists, poets, writers are jailed for speaking out. Indian newspapers print black-bordered sheets with no writing instead of bowing to censorship. It was less than thirty years ago that the chains of British colonialism had been cast off. A young, struggling nation is shocked to find that tyranny can be homegrown too.

In both countries, the young, as young people have done throughout history, take to the streets in protest.

The Continental Walk for Disarmament and Social Justice was a 'call for disarmament, a simultaneous shift of economic priorities away from militarism and toward meeting domestic and global human needs, and removal of the causes of war.'[146] The walk started in San Francisco in 1976 and ended many months later at the Pentagon in Washington,

D.C. with marchers joining in across the country, like streams to a mighty river. Eight thousand miles through thirty-four states.[147] Stalwarts from multiple fields sent a call to participate: Joan Baez, Richard Barnet, Noam Chomsky, Dorothy Day, James Douglass, Gloria Steinem and others.[148]

It was inevitable that Jo would join the Continental Walk. She was in college, and joined it in the summer of 1976. 'By then I felt I had done enough organizing and didn't want to walk. But someone insisted that I walk,' she recalls. 'I had such a great time. So, I decided, impulsively, that I would skip college and walk all the way to D.C.' The walk was a world of its own: everyone from Buddhist monks to war resisters and hippies, walking during the day, talking and planning deep into the night. The energy was extraordinary.

Jo's parents naturally supported the walk, but were worried that she would meet a boy at the Continental Walk, get married and never finish college. 'I said, "No way!"' Jo remembers with a big grin, 'I said the boys are so scruffy, with long hair, baggy clothes... no way.'[149]

The McGowans were a Catholic family who lived in Fall River, Massachusetts. Jo's parents had seven children. Large by today's standards, but not so uncommon in the 1950s.

Jo's grandfather, Patrick McGill, was Irish. He left home at the age of twelve, lacking a formal education, taking jobs wherever he could. He fought in the First World War and wrote poignantly about those tough times. His autobiography caused McGill to be banned from his village back home in Ireland because he criticized the church and its exploitation. 'Now, the village has a festival in his name,' laughs Jo, 'He's given them a claim to fame.' Jo's grandmother, Margaret Gibbons, was the great-niece of a famous cardinal in the Catholic church. After the Depression, Gibbons wrote enormously popular romance novels. Her circle of friends included the well-known writer, G.K. Chesterton, who became Jo's mother's godfather. 'My mother was brilliant; she was an intellectual like one rarely sees,' says Jo. As a young woman, Patricia McGill was focused on her career, with no time for romance. She moved to New York City, first as a telephone switchboard operator and then as a junior editor in a Catholic publishing house.

Jo's father, Owen McGowan, came from a working-class family. His father was a carpenter, his mother, a housewife. 'My father told stories of being hungry a lot, moving house multiple times, going to Catholic schools where he was sometimes taunted by the nuns,' Jo recalls. Yet, he was a staunch Catholic. In a true American Dream story, Owen went from dire poverty to being highly educated, earning a Fulbright scholarship and a PhD. He then started a Catholic bookstore.

'He was a terrible businessman,' says Jo. 'He never made money. He hated selling books and always wanted to give them away. The only thing that sold were the Hallmark cards and religious items, like what you need for first communion.'[150]

Owen went to New York City to buy books from a reputed Catholic publisher. He walked in, saw Patricia and said, 'That is the girl I want to marry.' Pat was enjoying her single life in New York – a combination of hard work, going out with friends and acts of charity. She didn't want to marry. They courted for years. Pat kept turning Owen down. 'We always wondered what made her finally say "Yes",' says Jo.[151]

Their bookstore failed, leading to bankruptcy. The McGowans were determined to pay off their debts. For years, their Christmas gifts to each other were paid-up bills. Their five-bedroom house with their seven children was like a Dr Seuss sketch, bursting at its seams. Yet there was always room for those in need. Three of Jo's grandparents lived with them. At one time, a young Catholic girl pregnant out of wedlock was thrown out by her parents. The

McGowans took her in. She came for a weekend and stayed with the baby for two years. The McGowans took in a neighbour who had mental health issues and nobody to look after her. A house on their street burned down, rendering its owner homeless. 'Go to the McGowans,' he was told, 'They will take you in.' And they did.

It wasn't all charity and sob stories. 'We weren't rich, but, in our childhood, we never felt poor at all. My father, given his childhood poverty, never wanted us to want for anything,' says Jo. 'They were the most wonderful parents. We grew up with a lot of laughter and excitement.' While there were no fancy vacations or expensive clothes, they had great holidays on beaches, and amazing parties at home. Her parents knew people like Dorothy Day and Seamus Heaney. Jo's mother went to hear Martin Luther King's 'I have a Dream' speech. By their actions, Jo's parents showed their children what mattered, what was important. You may be an ordinary person, but you can make a difference.

'I adored my parents and learnt so much from them,' says Jo. Money was always tight, but not generosity. At one point, there was literally no room at the inn, when Jo's uncle, who had thirteen children, called in a crisis. 'There was no space. It was winter. Friends got mattresses, blankets,' Jo remembers. 'And we had them for months. But for my mom it was the right thing to do. My parents always acted as though *they* were the lucky ones, being able to do the helping. They kept the dignity of the people they helped.'[152]

Her parents passed on to Jo the ability to see the good in everybody. Their actions taught her an important way of looking at the world, that people have many battles to fight, and we don't know the entirety of their story. 'My father would always say "Yes". And my mother would always say "I think that can be arranged,"' recalls Jo.

These are edicts she has carried into her work at Latika. 'I say "yes" to most of what the employees ask for, like extra days off. I don't mind having a reputation as a pushover,' she says. 'Because they feel a part of the organization. And, when I in turn ask them, they say "yes" and go the extra mile.'[153]

Mumbai, or Bombay as it was known then, was a smaller city in the 1950s. Its three million people – far fewer than today's twenty-one million – lived in neighbourhoods knitted together by the city's local-transit train system.

One stop on the rail line is Charni Road, where Ravi Chopra grew up. North of him was a large Maharashtrian population known for its raucously celebrated Ganesh festival. Farther up was Dharavi, one of Asia's largest slums, and then Bandra, with its churches and bakeries. South Bombay was where the wealthy lived: Fort, with its majestic British-era buildings, Malabar Hill's villas nestled in verdant gardens, and Nariman Point, the tip of the city, with bustling offices.

Ravi's father worked for the Indian government, moving around the country depending on what his job demanded. Ravi's mother, a teacher, was the linchpin of the noisy, busy household on Charni Road. 'We were financially comfortable, but there was no extra disposable income,' says Ravi. 'We are all brought up very thrifty, with few sets of clothes and lots of tasks per child.'[154] With his father travelling, a lot of the little jobs that are usually done by the man of the house became Ravi's responsibility. 'Going to the post-office, buying medicines, paying for and bringing in the groceries.' He was also given the responsibility, unthinkable these days, of shepherding a neighbour's three children from their building to their school thirty minutes away. He was ten; they were a few years younger.

As the first in the extended family to have moved to Bombay from Lahore, a few years before India's Independence, Ravi's parents' apartment was the base for all relatives who came to the big city seeking work. 'There were four of us children, and always lots of other people staying: cousins, uncles, aunts,' he says.[155] In such a set-up, there's seldom any notion of privacy or ownership of books or toys.

'Jo's family was similar. It is like that with us even now,' says Ravi with a grin. At one time in Dehradun, Ravi and Jo's house held the two of them, their three children, Ravi's aunt and mother. Add to this, long visits from Ravi's vast circle of relatives in India, and from the United States, Jo's siblings, their families, and Jo's parents. Visits measured not in days but months. 'We once had Dad, who was ninety, Mummy (Ravi's mum), who was ninety-five, Maasi (Ravi's aunt), who was eighty-five, Moy Moy, AND Latika!' says Jo with a grin.[156] It is astonishing, given the melee, that anyone got even the basics done, let alone set up and run two successful non-profits [Latika by Jo and the People Science Institute (PSI) by Ravi], and raise three children, as Jo and Ravi did.

One way to get things done is to have a strict schedule and stick to it. Ravi is legendary for his work ethic. At a desk that sits beneath the staircase at home, Ravi is up by 4 a.m., reading, writing, editing. 'As children, we were expected to study and work hard. That habit persists,' he says. If you are middle-class or poor in Bombay, the local trains are never far from your consciousness. Millions commute on them daily. The whistle and rhythm of a train on the tracks permeates the house. At Charni Road station the first train would arrive at 4.40 a.m. 'So, I would wake up and study. It was always a cheerful waking up,' Ravi says. 'I was happy to do so.'[157]

This cheerfulness lurks behind many layers in Ravi, popping out occasionally. Dunu Roy, a childhood friend (and son of Latika Roy), says, 'Ravi's laughter is under the surface. He has that twinkling wit. He laughs uproariously and slaps his thigh.'[158]

There's a natural contrast between husband and wife. Ravi is stocky. Jo is taller, lean and gangly. Her personality is extroverted, approachable, up for a laugh and an adventure. Ravi has little time for small talk and can come across as forbidding. Their organizations mirror these contrasts. Jo's Latika is viewed by all as a more carefree place to work than Ravi's more serious People Science Institute (PSI). PSI is also less prone to funding crises, far from unknown at Latika.

It would be easy, while listing these contrasts, to miss Ravi's twinkly eyes as he learns something new, or the wicked humour that comes through as he describes a messy political situation and its historical origins. At the age of seventy-five, he reads eight newspapers a day; down from ten, across the political spectrum, in two languages. Some of his humour is sartorial. Ravi dresses in bright colours, matching from head to toe. Yesterday was purple. Today, everything is bright green: kurta, socks, handkerchief and even the pen in his breast-pocket. On his head sits either a jaunty traditional cap from the states of Himachal Pradesh or Uttarakhand, or a matching bandanna. Over the years, his beard has grown long and white. He'd easily pass for one of Snow White's brigade.

Ravi grew up in an India that had newly won its freedom from the British. Those were heady days. Mahatma Gandhi, with his mesmerizing leadership and movement of non-violence, was a big influence. 'As a young kid, you are very impressionable,' says Ravi. His mother's uncle worked with Mahatma Gandhi and Lala Lajpat Rai. 'Later he was in the Bhoodan and Sarvodaya movement, and became a Member of Parliament,' says Ravi. 'He was my role model.' The young Ravi saw not just a deep dedication to building a new India, but also the humility that remained despite the high office. 'My uncle had all this power, fancy facilities, and yet he would carry his own bags, only take public transport ... very selfless,' recalls Ravi. Such impressions run deep. After graduating from one of the best engineering colleges, the Indian Institute of Technology, Bombay, Ravi and his friends felt, 'We are supposed to be the cream of India and we should be creating jobs, not looking for jobs.'[159] This public-spirited attitude has led Ravi to co-found or contribute to many influential organizations, including the Indians for Democracy, Front for Rapid Economic Advancement of India, Centre for Science and Environment, and, his own People's Science Institute. Each organization addresses a social need – helping villagers improve irrigation and sanitation, turning a spotlight on the growing environmental crises in a rapidly industrializing country, or helping villages in the Himalayan mountains preserve lakes, rivers and ancient waterways.

The late 1960s brought a rude awakening, a disillusionment in the political landscape of India. 'Everybody just loved Nehru, our first Prime Minister,' recalls Ravi. 'It was pure, simple love. Of course, his mistakes were there, but nobody cared. Then came two wars. Nehru died. [His successor] Shastri died, and all that hope evaporated,' he says.[160] There were no jobs. Poverty worsened and the heady days of independence and immense possibility gave way to strong-arm tactics and corruption in the government.

In 1975, when prime minister Indira Gandhi declared an emergency, postponed elections and suspended the human rights guaranteed by the Indian Constitution, Ravi was in the US, studying for a PhD in metallurgy at Stevens Institute of Technology. 'Sheer perseverance got him to the US,' says Nutan, Ravi's younger sister, who now lives in New Jersey. 'He was the first in the whole extended family to go to America. We have a photograph of thirty people, including young kids, going to the airport to see him off. He's in a suit, covered in garlands!'[161] Ravi, his friends, and his mentor, Professor Mehta, expanded an existing organization, Indians for Collective Action, to support non-profit organizations in India. They also set up Indians for Democracy, to raise awareness and money to help the democratic movement in India and the refugee crisis from the India–Pakistan war that led to the creation of Bangladesh.

A *New York Times* article that covered their protests names Ravi and others, including the activist (turned well-known professor at JNU, Delhi), Anand Kumar.[162] The journalist writes, 'Gradually and apprehensively, a growing number of citizens of India who live in the United States are speaking out against restrictions in their homeland imposed by the government of Prime Minister Indira Gandhi. They are a diverse group. Until recently, many of them shunned political involvement of any sort.'[163]

In true Bollywood style, and in keeping with who they are, Jo and Ravi's romance began at the intersection of two peaceful protest rallies. Unaware of what fate had in store, they were marching towards one another. Jo was on the Continental Walk from Boston to Washington D.C., protesting issues of nuclear proliferation, for the future of humanity. Ravi was marching from the Liberty Bell in Philadelphia to the United Nations building in New York City, for the future of democracy in India.

Girl meets boy, or what the movies call the 'meet-cute.' War Resisters League (WRL), one of the organizers of the Continental Walk, had offered to guide the Indians. 'A car comes screeching to a halt. A tall woman I have never met, bounds out and gives me a huge hug,' remembers Ravi. 'And I am thinking, "Oh god, they [the other Indians] are going to think I spend my time womanizing in the US!" She introduces herself as "I am Jo McGowan, the advance party from WRL to welcome you."'[164]

They walk, chat, spend a few hours together. Jo accompanied Ravi to an event organized by the Indian protesters. 'It was horrific; testimonials of all the terrible things that were happening in India under the emergency,' she says. 'Then, I had to leave.'[165]

The protests rallies are going their separate ways, and so must they. 'Before we parted I wrote her name, her parents' address, in a tiny book I carried in my shirt-pocket,' says Ravi. 'Then, she went on her walk and I on mine. That was it.'[166] (Remember, this was an era without e-mail and smartphones).

Jo and Ravi did not see each other for two years but they wrote. 'I remember getting this postcard from Ravi,' Jo says. 'Holding it and thinking, "Oh my god, this is the guy I am going to marry."'[167]

By the time Ravi visited the McGowans in 1978, Jo had forgotten what he looked like. And Ravi had forgotten what a large family Jo came from. 'It was hilarious,' says Jo. 'I had a bouquet of flowers, kept looking at any dark-skinned person approaching me and wondering, "Is it him?"' (Jo gets the reverse of this in Dehradun – especially in the early years, the locals would confuse her with the handful of other white women living there).

While the McGowans had lots of non-white friends, Jo was the first to date a non-white person. At the end of his visit, Jo ended up driving Ravi from Fall River, Massachusetts, back to his university in New Jersey. 'And on that drive, we decided to get married,' says Jo. 'We knew almost nothing about each other.'[168]

'They got to know each other mostly through letters,' laughs Mary, the sister who is closest to Jo – and the one responsible for bringing Moy Moy into her life. 'My parents were concerned. Jo got married so young, at twenty-one. Meeting Ravi's parents really helped my parents – to see their solid marriage.'[169] Flights were expensive and could only be afforded every few years. A move away from the United States was an enormous undertaking. 'My family liked Ravi but they were worried about my moving to India,' recalls Jo. 'My dad particularly was devastated. My mom said, "You have to live your life. You have opened the world to us. Now we have family there."'

Dan Berrigan, an anti-war activist priest, married them. Berrigan asked Ravi, 'What if Jo doesn't like India? Ravi said, 'Then we will come back.' 'Of course,' says Jo with a big grin, 'we never did.' They both worked to earn enough for the plane tickets and in 1981, they came to India. They had about four thousand rupees in their pockets. 'My father, a typical Indian father, was disappointed,' remembers Nutan, Ravi's sister, 'that his son was not coming back from America with millions.'[170] Sending a son abroad, in those days, was rare and a sacrifice. Ravi was coming back with nothing.

The early years were bumpy. 'It was awful for me,' says Jo. 'The heat, the constant noise, the chaos.' There was the loneliness of a foreigner sitting in a crowded room. Ravi's relatives would ask her,

'How do you like India?' in English and after that single question, switch to conversing with others in rapid Hindi or Punjabi. 'Nobody asked me about my dreams, my feelings ... Even Ravi didn't realize what was happening to me,' Jo says.[171]

Learning Hindi was a coup. 'She won over everyone,' says Nutan, 'They would say, "*Yeh to Hindustani bahu se bhi acchhi hui*" ("She is better than an Indian daughter-in-law").'[172] Jo echoes Nutan: 'That was the best thing I ever did, studying Hindi. It is the best investment anyone can make. Particularly in India where people are so encouraging.' Being able to speak Hindi brought Jo simple connections with ordinary people – the security guard at the airport, the maid in a friend's house, the vegetable vendor. 'The conversations are not deep, but it gives me such pleasure. The pleasure of human communication. It has given me so much insight into what true happiness is. I love it when I get a Hindi joke and can crack up. You realize how little it takes to have fun!'[173]

'I learnt that a happy marriage needs a good sense of humour,' says Ena Gaur. 'Jo and Ravi gave me such a fresh perspective of what a couple could be like – man not the sole bread-winner, wife not doing all the cooking. There is a sense of equality [between them]. They discuss everything. There is a core belief system,' Ena pauses. 'Most of all,' she says, 'I really like that both of them are so passionate about what they do.'[174]

A mixed-culture marriage brings many things to the relationship, from big issues like, 'What religion will we raise the children in?' to tiny details like pumpkin pie. Pumpkin pie is as American as you can get. In Ravi and Jo's household, the kids adored it. 'Moy Moy would throw her arms in the air and cheer,' remembers Cathleen. 'So, we still have pumpkin pie on her birthday, instead of cake.'[175]

To the outside world, Latika is Jo's organization, just as PSI is Ravi's. Two clearly separate domains. Lift up the historical corners of Latika, though, and Ravi's imprints are visible everywhere. Latika would not have taken off without Ravi's contributions to the planning, discussions and guidance. His country, his friends with their initial donations and in-a-crunch-funding, and more deeply, his mentorship of a wife thirteen years younger. Ravi has an unflinching ethical core that finds its counterpart in Jo. They have a call and response: do what is right, stand up against injustice, help others. These are not easy things. Their marriage deepened such commitments. Speaking out for the voiceless and for what is morally right – these are big strands in the McGowan–Chopra marriage. At every meal, with their children, grandparents and visiting friends, heads are bowed and a prayer is said. It encapsulates what Jo and Ravi stand for and what they have dedicated their lives to:

May those who are hungry have food.
And those who have food,
Hunger for peace and justice on Earth.

7

What is Worth Working On

Anne Bruce's family thought she had gone mad. Instead of gardening or doing something quiet in retirement, she was off to a strange country that none of them had visited! Anne had seen a small article of Jo's re-printed in the Royal College of Speech and Language Therapists' newsletter. 'I thought, hmm ... why not?' She kept writing to Latika offering her skills. Nobody replied. Finally, shaky contact was made. 'Pre-internet days, I barely had an address and no idea about whether anyone spoke English,' Anne says.[176] That one visit became multiple visits over seven years until 2013. Each time, Anne would stay at Latika for six months. She would bring younger colleagues as volunteers

– special educators, physiotherapists and speech therapists doing their apprenticeship.

The daily presence of professional, specialized and highly experienced individuals has a profound influence when you are a young non-profit organization scrambling for funds and confronting a dearth of professional talent in a small city. After decades spent working in speech and language therapy and training numerous students in special education in the UK's National Health Service, Anne Bruce was well equipped to bring order into Latika's chaos. 'I could look and say, "This we can look at, this we can't address. What is worth working on?"'[177]

Volunteers like Anne brought in the latest research and methods. For instance, Latika employees were shocked when Anne insisted on spending her first few weeks only observing the children and their interactions with the staff. Anne says visiting Indian therapists 'were very traditional and set in their ways. Looking at a speech and medical model rather than a language and social model. Looking at muscles [of the child] rather than interactions between children and parents.'[178]

When a young child begins to speak, she quickly learns to ask for things. But what if a child's disability includes no language? There is no conversational cue, no vocabulary to rely on to understand what she wants. Over the years, Anne trained three young

Latika staff members who went on to become vital in-house therapists. She taught them what to look for, what to do, and how to do it with patience. 'It is very important to give non-verbal children choice,' says Anne. For if a child cannot speak, then he cannot express what he wants, and it is easy for friends and family to make assumptions. The child gets no agency. For example, hold up the child's toy in one hand, and something neutral like a toilet-roll holder, in the other hand. Encourage the child to look at the toy that she wants. And then give her lots of positive feedback. "You saw the toy; you looked at it!" 'We did things like that endlessly,' says Anne.[179]

Another method is to help establish cause and effect. After a full day at Latika, Anne would go to the Chopra household and do this with Moy Moy. Using specialized software on a laptop, they would look at the screen together. 'The idea was to get her to press a switch to change the screen,' says Anne. 'In the beginning, she would hold my hand and push. It is a question of little by little. The feeling that they have some power ... and the hope that Moy Moy felt that if she could make her screen change, then by vocalizing to people around her, she could get to make other choices.'[180]

Anne's methods are still in use. It is 2022. Sunita Singh and her team work with some of Latika's most challenging children. Sunita describes one of the multi-level ways in which they increase communication between a child, his parents and eventually, the rest of the world. A child with several disabilities and no language may not know how to pick up a glass of water and drink. 'We have multiple prompts that we gradually phase out,' says Sunita. 'Physical prompt, then verbal prompt, then clue.' First, the muscles of the hand need to be strengthened so that the child can hold a steel glass of water. A physiotherapist works diligently with the child. 'Over a month, the child is able to hold a glass. That is when we start with the physical prompt. My hand next to her hand, helping her to lift and guide the glass to her mouth. Then, we remove the physical prompt, my hand, slowly. We move to the stage of only verbal prompt – where I say, "Hold the glass, don't drop the glass."' This is done every day, at Latika, and at home by the parents. In the final stages it is only the clue: 'The glass is placed in front of the child. And she knows – what is in it, how to pick it up and drink.'[181]

A non-verbal child used to hit his cheek with his fist. 'It became a wound, and we did not know why he was doing it,' says Sunita. 'One day, he took my finger and stuck it in his ear. It was full of wax and pus. He had not been able to tell us about the pain. Because of the pain, he had been hitting his face, lashing out at home, not letting his mother wash his face, or cut his hair.' The ear issue was soon resolved and led, in turn, to another lovely solution.

Fresh from their success with the non-verbal child's painful ear, Sunita and her team embarked on an ambitious project to tackle a challenge faced regularly by parents: hair-cuts. Many Latika children resist haircuts because they do not like having their heads touched. The team undertook what is called 'systematic desensitization,' a form of behavioural therapy that is usually employed to address anxiety disorders and phobias. 'We built a rapport with a local barber, spoke to him about disabilities, how a number of children don't like their heads being touched,' says Sunita. 'Then the children went to the barber shop. They watched, while their *teacher* got her hair cut.' Latika took the children to the barber three or four times. 'In one visit, he would only massage their heads. Then slowly, slowly, over the visits, he'd cut. Then we faded out. Now, the mothers take the children to the barber for hair-cuts!'[182]

Giving professional feedback was another of Anne Bruce's contributions. 'I think my initial comments gave them quite a shock. Up till then – and even now – they are used to visitors coming and saying "Wonderful!" but in my professional view I had to say what I saw.' Anne's methods, taught and passed on along with training lessons in the classroom, mentorship in person, and rigorous feedback, have kept Latika fresh, child-centric and welcoming.

An excellent way to learn what is going on is to go and see for yourself. To quietly observe, to notice behaviour. Anne Bruce would travel in the Latika school van. With every trip she noticed how the driver and Latika helpers treated the children. She also saw parents in action: 'I always wanted to know about the families and their attitudes,' she says. 'I would see the parent bring the child, saying goodbye to the child. That was quite valuable – some parents would just push the child, leave without saying anything. Some parents employed a servant to do the drop-off. Some parents gave a hug, said goodbye, waved.'[183]

Soft spoken and garrulous, Ajay Sharma is a doctor whose career-path came to him in a dream, surprising his parents, who expected him to become an engineer. Get him at a dinner party with a glass of wine, he'll close his eyes, hum a bit and then, effortlessly recite reams of beautiful Urdu poetry.

His is the classic immigrant story. After seventeen years in Bulandshahr, a small town near Delhi, he moved to Lucknow to study medicine. Next step, cold Scotland, working for the UK's National Health Service. He started in paediatrics, specializing in children with disabilities. He married a Scottish woman, had two children and settled in London, working as a neuro-developmental paediatrician. In 2016, he retired as the clinical director of community children's services at Guy's and St Thomas' Hospital. Seeking to volunteer in India after retirement, Ajay, impressed by the work at Latika and Jo's ethical and non-hierarchical approach, began to spend time there.

While India has reached the World Health Organization's suggested aim of one physician per 1000 for its 1.4 billion population, quality is patchy.[184] Most doctors, pressed for time, tend to lecture their patients, expecting blind obedience, especially if the patients are poor. At Ajay's first encounter with Latika's parents, he threw out the power-point presentation and lecture. Instead, he did something that those parents, seated on the ground in their well-worn clothes, had probably never encountered before from a medical doctor – he led a genuine conversation. 'I just became a facilitator. I said, "Let's ask questions by area – epilepsy, or eating, or autism." So, "In this area are there any questions?" Then one parent asked [a question]. "Are there any similar questions?" Then, had any parent faced this problem and solved it, and, "Can you talk about it?" The parents were listening closely. It was so powerful.'[185]

It's a technique that he started using every time he came to India to work with parents at Latika. 'After every contribution, or question, I would ask everyone to clap,' he says.

'I had this notion in my head that parents don't do much for their children with disabilities,' he recalls. 'Then I started seeing all these parents at Latika's assessment centre. Really, really poor parents. Talking to them, I found they were clever. They had a strong desire to help their child. That really took me by surprise. I went home and told everyone that this is prejudice on my part, and this is how prejudice is shaken.'[186]

Ajay's visits to Latika since 2014 have lengthened from a few weeks to months. Latika employees look forward to his arrival and fill his schedule with as much training and evaluation work it can hold. Yet, in each visit, it is the parents he emphasizes on. 'Some of the best experiences for me, have been around parents, yeah,' he says in an accent that has the questioning English lilt, along with remnants of Indian softness. 'I find it is somehow different here versus the UK. In the UK, it is my work; I do it almost in a copy-book manner. I am slightly watching my back, so I don't put my foot wrong, yeah? There are no emotional moments there – I am half listening, half working out my next steps. Here,

I feel free and connected. Here, there are moments where I feel like crying ...'[187]

Parents who have a child with a disability are forever tagged. Others might be known for their careers, volunteer work, baking prowess. But those with special children, will, for the rest of their lives, be known as 'those parents with a disabled child.'

They, in turn, are thrust into an alien culture, one with its own language, its own intricate medical vocabulary. The world of autism, of Down syndrome, of being Deaf, is another world, and it is one that the parent, did not ask to enter.

Savitha Purohit is young, slightly built and shy. Her son, Shivansh, is three years old, and has cerebral palsy. 'The birth was difficult, he was stuck and taken out by force,' Savitha says. 'He was in ICU for two weeks.'[188] When he was eleven months old, the family began to worry. Shivansh was not gesturing, not able to move much. Despite being poor, the parents went to multiple hospitals, spending a lot of money trying to find answers. Then the pandemic struck. They were home-bound.

In 2022, mother and son started coming to Latika. 'He could not control his neck, no hand movement, nothing. He used to just lie in one position,' Savitha says. 'Now he can sit, he can stand. Now he can pick up a rolled *roti* to eat – his grip is improving. He can crawl towards toys and food.'[189]

Savitha's schedule shows her fierce commitment. 'We first came to Latika for three days at a time, now we come five days of the week,' she says. If they did not have the free Latika van to bring them, it would take her more than two hours, changing buses, to get here. That's not the only challenge. Savitha's husband works 250 kilometres away. Leaving her family behind, she moved to the city for her son. She rents a small room for the two of them. 'I have never stayed in a place like this,' she says. 'My husband comes for ten days every two months. It is hard but we have to do it for our son. I had never worked or stayed on my own before.'[190]

'At Latika, they train us well, with a lot of love,' says Savitha. 'I didn't know about CP at all. Now I have learnt about it and other conditions. We come to Latika only for three hours – most of our time with our children is at home. So, Latika tells us to do more at home, with what we have there – *katori*, plate, toothbrush and toothpaste. I tell Shivansh the names of things, what is in the room, and he asks for them by looking.'[191]

After participating in the therapy session with her son, Savitha sits outside while Shivansh continues in school. This is where she meets other mothers, also waiting for their children. 'The friendships have really helped,' she says with a shy smile. 'We laugh, forget our troubles. We support each other. Only one who has gone through this can know what we are going through. I learn from the older moms. I didn't know anything. They tell me how much progress is possible. It keeps my hopes up.'[192]

Her son has emboldened Savitha in ways that would not have occurred otherwise. 'Now I can go everywhere on my own. I can take my son everywhere,' she says. Her family has begun to ask, "What is this Latika place? How long will you live alone, on your own like this?" 'They want quick improvements, as though it is a disease to be cured,' she says. Savitha looks up, her eyes shining with an inner strength, and says, 'But I see this huge difference: he can look after himself, move around, he is not scared anymore. And I ... I prefer my independence.'[193]

'Make parent empowerment a core way of working for Latika,' is the first recommendation in Ajay Sharma's report of an organizational evaluation.[194] 'For me that is the main point. All else is operational,' he says. 'I said, "You have to change this completely" – no tinkering. All parents say you are nice to them. That is not the point. You have to see that the primary reason is for Latika to support the parents, not the child. The child is almost secondary. You have to have a contract with the parent – you are a parent-support centre. Give up the notion that you are running a school. Jo was surprised by my emphasis. The staff was stunned.'[195]

Ajay feels that at Latika, the norm is still the view that skills reside in the trained staff, who, in turn, teach parents and children. He sees this as a 'dependency model.' "'I am going to teach the child. I am going to give the parents homework.' This attitude needs to change."[196] In 2014, Ajay and his wife, Louisa, a general practitioner, came to Latika. They used stories from their three decades of experience of working with families along with research and scientific evidence, to encourage the Latika employees to work more with the parents. In that visit, Ajay said, 'Your goal is to make the parents into therapists and special educators.'[197] Ajay and his wife showed that *how* the employees spoke was as important as *what* they had to say. That while parents certainly need techniques, they primarily need confidence and belief in their ability to help their children.

What Ajay is grappling with and urging Latika to consider, is 'co-creation.' In the business world, there are many companies that are considered co-creation champions. Co-creation refers to involving stakeholders, usually customers or employees, to participate right at the beginning when a process or project is being designed, or when problems are being tackled. The outcome is then valued by all those involved (not just by the service-provider).

Lego, the beloved manufacturer of brightly coloured toy-bricks for children, was in financial trouble by the 2000s. New leadership brought in change, including Lego Ideas – an open-source development and idea generation platform. Lego fans post ideas for new products on the online platform and get voted on. The most popular ideas are produced with the creator named on the packaging. They even get a small percentage of the sales. This co-creation means Lego creates an active customer base. The customers get a direct say in what is made. More than a million ideas have been generated, the most popular ones selling well and contributing to lift Lego out of its financial doldrums.[198]

Latika already takes a very family-centric approach (rather than a child-centric approach), to disability. Parents are closely involved in the assessment and therapy stages. There are special counselling sessions for mothers. There's a club for young adults, for siblings, and one recently started for grandparents. There's even time for the mothers to sit outside laugh, relax and swap stories while their children are at the Latika school. All of this, thoughtfully crafted to create a network of support. Ajay's dream of co-creating with parents would layer in well here. 'Once they tap into their own strength, their own power,' says Ajay, 'oh, then just stand back.'[199]

8

Nation-building with a Hundred People

'Gandhi said that in the UK there are six kinds of smiles – for the cleaners, for your kids, for the colleagues whom you don't like ... I can read it in one glance,' remarks Ajay, sipping tea at Latika on a crisp autumn morning. 'I was attracted to Latika because of its culture. Both India and the UK have very strong class structures – humiliating those lesser than you is a way of establishing your position. Latika is different.'[200]

Jo has built an organization founded on an adherence to ethics and mutual respect. She provides the context within which these things matter, and how strongly they are valued. 'It has to be demonstrated again and again,' she says. Her focus on egalitarianism, on supporting those who would otherwise lack opportunities, personally and professionally, is rare. There is faith in the employees regardless of their position in the organization's hierarchy. It in turn, begets loyalty and elicits effort that cannot be won by money alone. Ashok Mamgain, driver of a Latika school bus remarks, 'When I first joined, it was surprising and so nice, so hard to believe that we are all treated equal.' Such reciprocal faith provides a structure within which Latika, in turn, can steadfastly support the underdog.

Every now and then there comes a moment in an organization's life that provides a snapshot of what it stands for, where its moral compass points towards. For Latika, one such moment is the Pooja case.[201]

'Could you drop my girl off at her grandmother's?' asks the mother. The tutor, a young man who comes regularly to teach her son, agrees. They live in a small village. The grandmother's house is not far. Just to be safe, the mother sends her son along as well. Both children perch on the back of the tutor's bicycle and head out. In a bit, the tutor stops the cycle and sends the son home on an errand. He takes Pooja, a thirteen-year-old girl with an intellectual disability, to a field and brutally rapes her.

When Pooja makes her way home, her parents think she's had an accident and rush her to the local health centre. The rape is discovered and the family is sent on to the government hospital, an hour away, in Dehradun. The girl has told her parents about the tutor's assault, so they know who did it. It is a small village and the families know one another. The tutor's family is part of the local mining mafia. They have power and money. It takes an entire day to get the police to agree to the first step – filing an FIR (First Information Report). Given the tutor's family's power, no arrest is made.

'India has great laws to protect children from sexual violence,' writes Jo in a blog-post. 'Just don't expect them to work. At least not on their own. Especially if you happen to be a girl. Or poor. Or disabled. If you are unlucky enough to be all three, you really, really, really need a friend in court.'[202]

That friend, for this young girl turned out to be Rizwan Ali, Latika's legal advisor. Jo heard of the case through the Dehradun Disability Forum, a coalition that brings together organizations in the city that work on issues of disability. Rizwan plunged in. 'The parents were clearly out of their depth,' Jo recalls. 'Poor, non-readers, cowed by authority and devastated by what had happened to their daughter, they seemed unable to even process the reality of the rape, let alone deal with it. The child was bewildered and in pain. She had lost huge quantities of blood and required multiple stitches.'[203]

Pooja was under tremendous strain with the constant questioning. She had a fifty per cent mental disability, with a certificate to vouch for it. Three people from Latika went to the hospital: Rizwan, Mamta Govil, a Latika Board member, and Rashmi Rangarajan, a psychologist. There, with gentle questioning and the use of a doll, they were able to get more of the story. The father, a rickshaw puller, sat in the hall, weeping.

It was 2012, and a new law, the Protection of Children from Sexual Offences (POCSO) Act had just been passed in the Indian Parliament. Rizwan, the police and the government were all new to the use and implications of the Act. As in other countries, the Indian government provides the victim with a lawyer. 'But under POCSO, the victim can also appoint her own lawyer,' explains Rizwan. So, Latika stepped in. Bizarrely, the government appointed a sign-language interpreter (for a child with a mental disability who understandably didn't know sign language).

Latika insisted that since Pooja's speech might seem slurred, the girl's mother was best suited to interpret it. Rizwan quickly gathered a team – a lawyer (himself), a psychologist (Rashmi) and someone to talk to the higher authorities (Jo). 'So, the victim's family had a one-stop shop, they didn't need to go anywhere else for their questions,' Rizwan says.[204]

The tutor was arrested only after Latika called up a senior police officer, who in turn called the inspector in charge of the case and insisted that an arrest be made. In the village, the tutor's family was desperately trying to prove that he was a minor, so that he would face lesser charges. They produced two certificates for his age, one saying he was fourteen, the other that he was seventeen. Both were accepted.[205]

At multiple points, it is clear that if it were not for Rizwan's energy and Latika's commitment to justice, the case would have fallen apart. The situation was as lop-sided as it could get. Pooja's parents lacked the social connections or the money that the perpetrator's family possessed. From the beginning, the tutor's family exerted tremendous pressure on the girl's family and on Rizwan. They threatened, offered money, tried to settle out of court and repeatedly tried to make the whole thing go away. Rizwan and Latika were dogged. He visited the family multiple times to explain things (a four-hour round-trip). He met numerous police officers, lawyers and government officers, spending long hours outside their offices waiting for a meeting. As the girl's appointed lawyer, he went to court at least thirty times. Most poor families do not receive such support, their cases easily buried and ignored.

Rizwan's work on this case had far-reaching ramifications. Following protocol, the girl's clothing had been taken for testing but DNA samples had not been collected. When Rizwan insisted (going again all the way to the highest-ranking police officer in the state), it was done ... but how? Not only were the victim, her mother and the accused brought together in front of the magistrate for the procurement of samples, but they were brought there in the same car![206] This was in clear violation of an Indian Supreme Court ruling which guarantees that a child who has been sexually attacked will not have to see the perpetrator in the courtroom.[207] 'We told the police about the ruling. The state government then passed an order so that all investigating officers in the future would know this, so that it would not happen again. It was a landmark issue,' Rizwan recalls.[208]

The second far-reaching impact was the fight for monetary compensation. At the end of six long months, Pooja's case was resolved. It took another two years for the government's compensation money to materialize – unwaveringly, eye-wateringly boring work on the part of Rizwan and his legal intern at Latika. 'So many procedures needed to get done,' he says. 'We learnt so much. For example, applying for compensation has to be done in the first six months. The family is poor. They don't have a bank account. So, a bank account had to be opened to receive the compensation. Now, if the parents are illiterate and the child is disabled, who operates the account?'[209] It turned out that the account could be operated by both parents, or a legal guardian. The bank refused to do this, since it was not the norm, and possibly involved extra paperwork. Finally, the bank had to agree because Rizwan showed them that legally, the bank could not say no. While pushing for her money to come through, Rizwan was able to free up not just Pooja's compensation of two hundred thousand rupees[210] but the compensation money of *sixteen* other victims. This money had been in bureaucratic limbo for years. It was the first time such an event had occurred in the state of Uttarakhand.

Working with what you have, rather than wishing for what you lack, is a trait that has stood Latika in good stead. A company or organization while hiring asks: How many degrees does he have? Where did she study and train? How well can he communicate in English? 'At Latika, a staff-member might only have a high-school degree, but she will be highly skilled,' says Ena Gaur. 'Jo has gotten them to train in a specialty, and they have been at Latika for many years.' Emphasize the values, then provide training for the skills that a person needs. Do it in the local language. Latika has done this repeatedly, with its special educators, teachers, physiotherapists, child development aides and drivers. 'They know how to put a family at ease, how to put a child at ease,' says Ena.[211]

Shivani Kapoor is not someone who disappears in a crowd. Today, she's in a maroon, hand-block printed salwar-kameez, her round face anchored by a beautiful *bindi* on her forehead. She remembers the exact date she joined: the fifth of June, 1995. The day it opened, Latika had four employees: Paula Hughes, Shaila Faleiro, Manju Singhania and Shivani Kapoor. Outspoken and cheerful, Shivani not only knows the children in her care, she also possesses institutional knowledge that stretches back to Latika's origins. She bustles around with a quiet force and a smile that comes from having grown with the organization in skill and spirit.

That spirit took many knocks along with way. Shivani grew up in a poor household. After school she was determined to work. 'I was the first girl in our family who worked. I had to fight a lot,' she says.[212] They couldn't afford to buy a daily newspaper, so she'd go to the local library to search for jobs. One day, she saw an advertisement from Latika. Jo and Ravi interviewed Shivani multiple times to make sure she wanted to be with Moy Moy and help set up Latika. Given how young she was, they even visited her home and spoke to her parents to ensure support.

The boundaries in the early days between home and organization barely existed. On some days, along with looking after Moy, Shivani would go door-to-door picking up children with disabilities for Latika's programmes. On other days, she'd help paint awareness posters – doing whatever was needed. 'Jo didi sent me for trainings,' she says. 'I learnt a lot about how to involve children with disabilities in activities, through play, how to understand their emotions.'[213] All that Shivani had absorbed naturally during the time she spent with Moy Moy was thus fitted into an academic framework.

'Ravi bhaiya would say to me, 'Don't bring your tiffin. Just think that you are coming to spend time with your other family during the day," she remembers with a smile. 'He would insist I sit at the table with them for lunch. We'd share our food.'[214] This tiny detail, employer and employee eating lunch together, might seem unremarkable. In a country with crevasses based on religion, caste and class, it isn't. It is not unusual, even today, to see, as journalist Tripti Lahiri writes, 'a couple seated with their child at a table for four, while the help is dispatched to sit not one but two tables away.' Lahiri goes on to say: 'Borders between countries are marked out by fences and guards, but borders between classes are marked out by where you may sit, where you may go to the bathroom, and where and with whom you may eat.'[215]

There is little upward mobility in most non-profits. In a 2022 survey that canvassed more than 400 non-profit organizations in the United States, with budgets from $1 million to $100 million, forty-three percent of employee turnover was found to be due to 'lack of opportunity for upward mobility or career growth.'[216] Often, a clear divide separates field staff and management. Field staff work at the front-lines, typically in the local language; managers draw up strategy, interact with donors and run meetings, typically in English. Latika is a strong counter-example.

What do you do if you are in a small town with few professionals in your area of operations? If you have no business plan and practically no money? You cobble together what you can. You look for diamonds in the rough and polish them till they sparkle. Shivani could be the poster-child for mobility within an organization, for breaking through what would be glass barriers anywhere else. She went from being Moy's helper to assistant teacher in a Latika classroom. Then she started managing a class, became a teacher herself. Now, she's a senior special educator. 'Jo is very generous about training employees – their time, finding the funding to pay for training,' says Anne Bruce.[217] Ummeed in Mumbai runs well-regarded training programmes for those in the field of disabilities. Since its inception, Latika has sent close to twenty employees, including Shivani, there for training that can go from weeks to months.

Moving between centres happens quite frequently at Latika. 'Some people put their hand up and ask for it; others we move,' says Jo. 'It gives them a new perspective; they perform better.'[218] Shivani moved too. Over the years, she has worked at all the Latika centres, including heading the vocational training centre for a while, learning at every stage. She had Jo's help at work and the unstinting support of her husband at home. 'I did my graduation and then some years later my B.Ed. (a requirement for teaching),' she says. 'My mother-in-law protested, but my husband filled my forms, did everything that was needed. I only had to study and take the exams.' Her desire to learn is palpable. There's a sizzle in the air when she talks about it. 'After B.Ed., I learnt sign language. Then a foundation course in special education. All paid for by Latika,' she says. 'And now, I want to specialize within special education – in learning disabilities, how to detect it, how to help, maybe even,' here her seriousness gives way to a twinkle in the eye, 'maybe even out of Dehradun somewhere.'[219]

Some of the Latika diamonds are easy to overlook. Most office and apartment buildings in India have *chowkidars*, young men who provide some sense of security by their physical presence at the entrance, but actually spend most of their time recording visitors' names or accepting deliveries. At Latika, Jo appointed two young women. It was unheard of – female *chowkidars*! 'Anita and Nisha are so good,' says Jo. 'One stays at the gate; another goes to all the corners in the evening and checks (that all is well). Such role models!'[220]

9

The Obsession with Scale

'I have never wanted to get gigantic,' says Jo. 'Because there is something really weird about walking into a place that is full of disabled children. It is not human scale, it is institutional. I hate it. This came to me right at the beginning – when we were seven or eight children (at Latika). I walked in with Moy Moy and thought, "Moy is not like that! They are disabled." Of course, Moy was in some ways more disabled, but to us, she was just Moy Moy. In a big group, you can't see the individuals.'[221]

Everyone loves a non-profit model that grows quickly (or 'scales,' to use the term insiders favour). Donors have a soft spot for it. Growth makes for a great story. An organization that started in one small town and, thanks in part to their support, now operates nationwide. Every year, numbers go up: people reached, staff hired, training sessions conducted. Growth justifies more funding. It provides a talking point for the funders, and something for the organization to boast about. 'I can get quite nasty about this obsession,' says Ravi, with a chuckle. (He has spent years supporting individuals or small organizations that work locally on issues of the environment and democracy.)[222]

Latika's vision statement reads, 'To provide specialized, *localized* services to children with disabilities and their families, and help others do the same.'[223] Latika has remained in Dehradun. While it has outreach programmes within the state of Uttarakhand, it has no offices in other cities or states. Thus far, Latika has brought comfort and skilled assistance to thousands of families. Every year it provides an increasing number of children with much-needed services. Through training sessions, workshops and awareness initiatives, it reaches almost 5,000 people annually in remote areas of northern India.[224] One could ask, "Why not more?" or one can pause to consider all those who may not have received much-needed, high quality care and guidance had Latika not existed.

Latika was named one of India's ten best organizations in developmental disabilities, singled out for its 'exceptional work.'[225] It is clear that the pool to be helped is immense – the report that lauded Latika also noted that 12 per cent of Indian children between the ages of two and nine have developmental disorders (approximately 44 million children)[226] – but is the burden solely on Latika to do so?

Decades ago, in a book, *Small is Beautiful*, the economist and journalist E.F. Schumacher made the case that when it comes to economic, social and environmental policy and practice, bigger is not always better. What's noteworthy is his book's subtitle: *A Study of Economics as if People Mattered*. 'As if people mattered' is Latika's mantra. It doesn't matter if you are poor and only speak the local language, you as a parent will be listened to. You will learn that what your relatives think is weird in your child actually has a medical name, and you will be shown what needs to be done for her to grow well and blossom.

Sunita Chauhan, a Latika parent says, 'We are so lucky that our city has Latika! I have seen other families struggle. Parents are an easy target for others to make money. People come from faraway cities – there are mothers who move here because of Latika. They leave their village, their whole family, and come here.'[227] Sunita learnt to drive a scooter, and, more recently, a car – all to help her second child, Mannan, who is autistic.

When her son was nine months old, Sunita was visiting her family in a small town in Punjab. An aunt pointed out that Mannan was not responding to his name. 'I was so scared. We didn't know anything about disability then,' she says. They went to see a well-known local doctor. 'He [must have known that] Mannan was a special needs child, yet all he told us was, "The child's ears and eyes are fine."' If he had diagnosed Mannan earlier, we would have caught things earlier,' says Sunita, the memory spurring a rage still present eight years later.[228]

When Mannan was three, his grandfather took a sick cousin to Doon hospital. Mannan went along for the ride. The doctor sent them to Gubbara (the Latika assessment centre housed, at that time, within Doon hospital). At Gubbara, he was observed for almost three hours. 'I was so anxious,' says Sunita, who was waiting at home. 'The cousin was sick, so why were they examining *my son*?'

After assessment and diagnosis, Sunita was asked to go to Latika's Early Intervention Centre (EIC). 'We thought it will take six months to fix,' she says frankly. Then she started reading and learning more about autism from Latika. 'I got so frightened. There is so much on the internet, too. My son looks normal, you can't tell at all, by looking at him ... How is it possible that he has a disability?' Sunita was a teacher at that time, and had seen some children with physical disabilities at her school. 'I am educated, we are middle-class and yet, I did not know anything about this disability,' she says, in shock. 'How could it be possible?'[229]

With diagnosis came the reaction of the extended family. Sunita's in-laws wanted her to go to other doctors, get multiple medical opinions. All the doctors said, 'Go to Latika, it is the best.' Sunita remembers friends and neighbours telling her, 'To do pujas, that our earlier karma was coming back to haunt us, that we have to suffer for the faults of our earlier lives.'[230]

'Latika has changed Mannan so much,' says Sunita. 'Earlier he used to hit himself, sit in a corner and not interact with anyone. He didn't know how to use the toilet and would soil his clothes wherever he was. We couldn't take him anywhere.' Through therapy, class and working at home, things changed. Latika made Mannan a head-cap to protect his head and crown from his fists. It eased the hitting. Toilet training meant Sunita's in-laws now take Mannan everywhere – to tea with relatives, to weddings, to the park. Sunita learnt from the therapists not just how to do things for her second son but for herself and her first son (who does not have a disability). 'I slowly learnt how to be peaceful at home for Mannan,' she says quietly.[231]

Mother and son have been coming to Latika for seven years. Sunita is involved in the mothers' group, and now, the siblings group. 'I am quite concerned for special children's siblings,' Sunita says. 'Mannan's older brother feels Mannan is behaving like this on purpose. Or that the disabled one is more favoured.' Sunita has brought her older son to Latika for counselling and to participate in the siblings group. 'He gets embarrassed, even though his friends are okay with Mannan. I show him other siblings at Latika, those whose brother or sister have other disabilities. "See how that sibling is being supported?" We explain that we have to create our own circles – if we do not take Mannan into society, who will?'[232]

Heading over to pick up her son from school, Sunita turns at the door and says, 'All parents of special-needs children want a miracle, a *chamatkaar*. At Latika we learnt that it happens, but slowly.'[233]

'We thought it unethical to only diagnose and not follow up with families,' says Shubha Nagesh, a doctor and the former head of research at Latika. 'We needed to understand what is going on with the kids we assessed, how their home plans were working out.'[234] Families were seeking Latika's services from far-flung villages nestled in the surrounding foothills of the Himalayas. They were arriving from cities like Allahabad, 800 kilometres away. Many were poor or lower middle-class. Word of Latika's high-quality and affordable care had spread. Reaching the organization meant losing a day's wages, taking one or two buses for several hours, using precious savings for tickets, food and other expenses. Faced with such barriers, a family might make the effort once, for diagnosis, to understand what their son or daughter has, but they may not return for repeated sessions of counselling, therapy and training.

So, Shubha and her colleague, Dr Sebastian Gruschke decided that if the families could not come, Latika would reach the unreached. They set up an experimental eighteen-month programme, funded by Sight Savers International. 'We'd go to the government facilities in each district,' recalls Shubha.[234]

At the heart of India's public health system sits the Accredited Social Health Activist (ASHA) worker. Launched in 2005 as part of India's National Rural Health Mission, the idea was to have an ASHA worker in every village. She lives locally and builds ties between the community and government health services. Her purview includes encouraging safe birthing practices, providing information on immunization, and keeping basic health and demographic records. Latika decided to tap into the ASHA worker network to reach families with disabilities. Latika trained them, gave them stipends, created a book in the local language – all to teach them how to identify babies with disabilities and how to support the families. The World Health Organization has a list of questions to investigate at every birth. Trained to use this list, the ASHA workers could screen, propose early diagnoses, and direct children with disabilities to Latika.

Latika gives poor and middle-class families multi-specialty care under one roof, something even the wealthy lack. It decided to take this same approach to the hard-to-reach. If daily or weekly intervention is not possible, how do we make *something* possible? They cannot come to us; can we go to them?

Doctors, physiotherapists, special educators, child-development specialists and legal experts came together to form the Latika outreach team. They joined forces with local disability-organizations and government workers. They went to villages and towns, performed assessments and follow-ups. They sketched out home-plans and built support networks for parents. What was sustainable in the long-term? What would help the most? The team shaped their work around these questions and not 'What would benefit Latika the most?'

This kind of outreach made a tremendous difference. Families no longer felt alone. They could turn to neighbours, their local government and Latika for support. Children with disabilities finally had specialized, targeted help. Latika didn't stop here. Once a month, Latika would cover the cost of transportation to Dehradun.

Children on home-plans began to turn up: first fifty, then a hundred. 'It was like an ashram,' says Sebastian. 'We could see the children over a week – every day they would come to the centre, and we would do tests, exercises, talk to parents, give information. They would come on Monday and by Friday, we would have a report ready, in Hindi and English.'[235] This, in turn, reinforced other important components of Latika's work, like data and research. Latika could track the extent to which its services were helping. 'It is now a full-fledged, well-developed programme,' says Shubha. 'Our staff are fully involved. They are seeing the impact of outreach.'[236]

Like the government, the Indian armed forces have extensive reach. The Indian Army has numerous dedicated services for its employees all over the country, including schools for special-needs children (also open to local children with disabilities). The Army has thirty-nine such schools. Aarti Nair, Director of Services, was married to an Army officer and ran the Latika-Army partnership. 'The President of the Army Welfare Association asked us for a proposal. This led to an evaluation of all the Army's special schools and then a specialized training,' says Aarti. 'It was tailored so we could address all the gaps that the evaluation found.' The exercise spanned sixteen months.[237] Through this partnership, Latika helped more than 1,500 families and trained more than 460 therapists and educators.[238]

Outreach programmes extend Latika's reach. As does public speaking. Jo has been an invited speaker at TEDx talks, the India Inclusion Summit, and numerous national-level conferences. She is the recipient of awards like the CNN IBN Real Hero award, the Laadli Award from Population First and the *Times of India* Icon Award. Latika has received awards like the Sightsavers International Innovative Project Award and the NGO of the Year Award from the National Trust. In 2022, Latika was one of a hundred organizations to be chosen as a changemaker for the prestigious EdelGive-GROW grant for which more than 3,000 had applied. Jo is well-known among policy makers, donors and non-profits that work in the disability field.

Similarly, Sandeep Khanna and Rizwan Ali have been invited to join government committees and asked for their thoughts on policy. All this means that Latika's voice, its message about the need for awareness of and integration of disability, reaches an audience far larger than the local population it serves.

A third way of addressing the issue of scale is to build a model so remarkable that parts of it are irresistible to emulators in other places. Jo says, 'We were a big part of the importance of a family-centred approach for early intervention.' Latika's Gubbara, the assessment centre's presence in a large public hospital, was a first in the country. 'Government officials from all over came to see it,' says Jo. 'There was an influential neonatologist from Calcutta who was encouraging early intervention all over the country. His was a medical-heavy approach and he often was at loggerheads with us. He said he had to acknowledge our way even though his bias was towards a more medical approach.'[239]

Latika has also contributed to public–private collaborations. It was appointed as the lead agency to train medical and educational staff, and to help establish EICs at the district level in the state of Uttarakhand. As a UNESCO report states, 'This improved the government's capacity, and marked an important step towards early identification and accessibility for families with special children living in rural districts across the state.'[240] Latika's EIC has been replicated as a model: Ummeed is one of India's leading NGOs, respected for its work in the field of children with disabilities. Ummeed's Child Development Centre is modelled on Latika's EIC. Ummeed, in turn, provides consulting services to other organizations, including in 2020, early intervention training at the Fernandez Child Development Centre, a unit of the Fernandez Foundation. So, the Latika model from northern India, has travelled to Ummeed in western India, and to Fernandez in southern India. Such influence is not easy to measure, but its impact is keenly felt. It is scale of a different kind.

10

A Matter of Faith

'The only way to come to terms with tragedy,' wrote Cathleen, Jo and Ravi's middle child, when she was nineteen, 'is to accept that it is a part of God's bigger plan, and that there is a purpose to all that He does ... I've seen it work in my own family. This is a truth people spend time searching for, but families like mine ... are lucky to have been blessed with experiences that, heart-breaking as they may be to live through, have taught us so much about life, acceptance, faith and love.'[241]

There is a quiet and deep sense of community that comes with faith. It steadies. It anchors. It reminds us of a world beyond ourselves and our troubles, acting as a ray of promise, gossamer thin perhaps, but shimmering nevertheless.

One of the strengths of India is the richness of its diverse religious fabric. Nowhere is this more apparent than in mixed marriages. While the Indian census does not record inter-faith marriages, about 3 per cent are thought to be mixed.[242] A mulching of practices arises: Muslim wives who know more *Bhagavat Gita* verses than their Hindu husbands. Christian husbands who don't cook meat at home out of respect for their pure vegetarian, Jain wives. Homes where all religious festivals are celebrated: Holi, Eid, Diwali, Christmas. In the early years of their marriage, Ravi had said to Jo, in words that are now famous in the family, 'You can do what you want. Baptize the kids, bring them up Catholic... (pause)... anyway, they will be Hindu!' What Ravi was getting at was the substance of cultural amalgamation. So, while Jo took her three children to church and did in fact have them baptized, the family also had Sikh and Hindu influences from Ravi's family. 'We found, over time, more than religion, it is your values that shape the family,' says Jo.[243]

'I don't know how much hyperbole is allowed for one's own parents, but shall we start with the word "Saints"?' exclaims Anand, Jo and Ravi's son. 'They are both fiercely driven, idealistic activists.

They recognize that a lot of success in anything, especially in non-profits, comes from diligence and persistence. The joke [while I was] growing up,' he says, 'was that there was always someone awake at home – Mom's up till 2 a.m. and Baba wakes up at 3 a.m.'[244]

Cathleen and Anand have seen hard work, discipline and rigour in action. 'My parents work so hard. They were always thinking about their work. We talked about it at lunch, dinner, on our walks. It served as a great model for us. They did it in a way that everyone was a part of it,' Cathleen says. 'One of the things I learnt was how you need to translate what you do in your profession to your family. They have set up this casual, easy way of taking big concepts and make them relevant to everyone,' she says.[245]

Such a strong work ethic could easily get in the way of being hands-on parents. Where's the time to transmit values to children? 'They are very dedicated parents. They believe in education, strong family support and helping people. All of that flows into their parenting,' says Anand. He remembers a time in high school when he was struggling academically. 'I would go with Baba to the office. He would be working. I would do my school assignments and he would tutor me. So even with the amount of work that they took on, it didn't hold them back in being very present parents.' Anand has a young son, and a busy job at an online education company. While Ravi and Jo's dedication felt normal in his childhood, now, looking back, it boggles his mind. 'I would really struggle to make that kind of time,' he admits.[246]

With the same dedication, Ravi and Jo created a world for Moy Moy. It is a fact that everyone remarks on. How Jo would take Moy *everywhere*. How Ravi engaged with his 'little angel.' How even when Moy Moy turned non-responsive she was included in the family drawing room, at the dining table, and on all social occasions.

Jo approaches the right to life issue from an uncommon angle, that of disabilities. 'Individual families may have concerns about the challenges of raising a child with autism or Down syndrome, and I understand that,' she says. 'But if you look at it at a macro level, it can easily look like a national programme of determining who should live ... It becomes political, very quickly.'[247]

There is a preciousness to life not captured by policy. History has shown us the dark underbelly of movements that focus on creating a perfect race and their devastating consequences. With increased testing at pregnancy, could we end up living in a world that has no children with disabilities? The medical world is rife with debate as the scope and capability of pre-natal screening expands. Those in favour argue that it can 'avoid suffering' for the psychological and social well-being of the child, the parents and society.[248] Disability-rights groups see such pre-natal screening and the abortions that may follow as discriminatory; sending a signal that those with disabilities, 'are a burden on "the rest" of society, and therefore, unwelcome.'[249] 'Even "normal" or "perfect" babies grow up into ungrateful adults alienated from their families, or get addicted to drugs ... So, who is to say what is good to have?' Jo argues. 'It is not a simple stance.'"[250]

As the mother of three children, especially one who had increasingly severe disabilities, Jo's words are filled with experience, heartache and love when she says, 'I really, really feel that the existence of people of all kinds makes the world more interesting and more fun. Disabled, particularly intellectually disabled, children bring us joy but also so much pain, [they] hamper our lives. I know that *so* well,' she pauses and adds, 'Every single life comes with challenges and joys.'[251]

The *Commonweal*, a nearly-100-year-old magazine, reaches those in the Catholic tradition. Jo has been a columnist since 1999, covering everything from Indian politics to trash collection to the exclusion of women priests in the church. In a piece titled 'Why I Stayed and Why I am Leaving,' she writes:

> 'I had been putting my faith in an institution whose time is up, in rituals that no longer serve any purpose and in hierarchies that have lost credibility.
>
> This institution and many of its rituals grew out of the very things Jesus rejected most stridently; the Gospel accounts repeatedly show him subverting hierarchy and upending the religious pecking order. He lambastes the priests for loving power and authority more than justice and mercy. The people he likes live out on the margins, and while they may not be educated or know the language, their values are clear. The Samaritan drawing water from the well, the leper who said thank you, the bleeding woman who had the faith and the nerve to defy her culture and approach him – these were his people.'[252]

Not throwing the baby out with the bathwater, Jo has moved away from the structures of the institution – she has rejected the power, hierarchy, and wealth of the Catholic Church – but her faith remains true. 'I believe in Jesus, but also Guru Nanak, and other spiritual teachers,' she says. Jo's mother had a good way of putting it, 'Divine power is like an electric current. Some people are plugged into it, and make it available to the rest of us.'[253]

The belief in something greater than oneself, leads to occurrences that aren't easily explained. The big decisions in Jo's life fall into this category. 'I cannot explain, for example, marrying Ravi. It was something outside of me, a force that I was going along with.' A similar feeling occurred with the decision to adopt Moy Moy. 'I knew she was premature, and there might be problems on the way,' Jo says, 'it just felt like *this* is decided.'[254]

Jo used to pray regularly. Over time, Moy Moy became her prayer. 'Taking care of her, especially in the later years where there was no response to the bathing, the feeding, the walking ... not even a smile,' she says. It is easy for the routines to become mechanical, all effort and no response or reward. 'We are taught in the Church that there will be dry spells, but just pray anyway. The rewards are intangible, but they keep building. For ten years, it was like that with Moy,' she says softly. Sometimes she would sense that feeling of prayer in others. 'I'd watch Ravi when he prepared Moy's food – measuring, mixing the formula, getting it all lined up

– he would take much longer than me, it was such a special moment.' And sometimes those intangibles would bear startling, deeply moving rewards. 'When I really paid attention, there would be a look from Moy to me – a connection.'[255]

Latika works for and among people whom all sacred traditions embrace: those rejected by society, those laughed at, those misunderstood and scorned. Latika's work brings them into the fold. 'You belong; you there, you also belong; and so, do you, all of you,' Latika whispers to the girl with cerebral palsy, to the boy with mutism, to the children with severe autism. Jo's moving away from institutionalized religion did not lessen her faith, it freed her to tap into something vaster.

'I am a little pencil in God's hands,' said Mother Teresa. It is one of Jo's favourite quotes:

> 'I am a little pencil in God's hands. He does the thinking. He does the writing. He does everything and sometimes it is really hard because it is a broken pencil and He has to sharpen it a little more.'[256]

This feeling of not being alone, of being an instrument in the larger scheme of things has always been present for Jo. It is not necessarily the belief in a particular God, but a fuller, deeper connection with something beyond the individual. 'It gives me support when I am really sad,' she says. 'Somehow there is a feeling of the universe around me, that I am not alone. And my small issue is a piece of something much, much larger. It diminishes the pain. I feel the wider community.'[257]

When Jo is away, her office is used for privacy and meetings. A colleague walks in. The white board behind him is covered with numbers in green and red, the red dominating. Unperturbed, he waves a hand and says, 'Oh, Jo looks after all of *that*.'

That is money: fund-raising and the annual budget. No one in Latika seems to worry or wonder where the money comes from. There's complete confidence in Jo didi raising the needed funds year after year. Jo jokes about how the staff view her: 'Mom is great; she brings in the money!"'[258]

There are a handful of non-profits in India that do not struggle for funding. They tend to be large, with multiple offices across the country, working on causes that are easy to understand: nutrition, primary education, skills training. For most non-profits, however, funding lurches from year to year between a hope and a prayer.

Jo's approach to funds for Latika has, over the years, driven many people bonkers. Her husband, her board members, her close friends, all have been appalled, flabbergasted or worn-out by what seems, to put it mildly, to be an eccentric approach. Fund-raising for Jo has always been a different kind of faith, one that is not for the faint-hearted. Her attitude – and the title of a talk she gave some years ago – is: 'Leap and the net will appear.'[259] To the chagrin of all the systematic people in her life, when Jo leaps, financial assistance does seem to show up!

'Any giving is giving,' says Jo. 'I sincerely believe that. There's plenty to do and we cannot do it alone.'[260] So, whether it is animals, or children in the street, or Latika and its children with disabilities, Jo encourages people to donate even if it does not directly benefit her organization.

The desire for a permanent building for Latika is a prime example of Jo's faith. Latika and Ravi's organization, PSI, both acquired plots of land in 2000. By 2017, PSI had finished building. The Latika land lay brown and dusty, not a single brick laid. NGOs are always scrambling to make ends meet. With most of the money going into programmes and projects, there is little left for beauty. 'I wanted our building to be a shining example, not falling apart, no Indian jugaad.' Jo says.[261] The Latika building would be a beacon for disability-friendly use, beautifully designed by expert architects and constructed by excellent builders. So, while PSI put up a building (lovely in its own way), moved in and got on with work, Latika continues in rented premises, its dream building relegated to delicate blue-pencil designs on rolled-up sheets of architectural paper.

Cushman and Wakefield, the international commercial real-estate services firm, agreed to execute the Latika building project. They waived their fees, but money was still needed for construction. 'Where's the money, Jo?' they asked at each meeting. 'The money will come,' Jo replied, every time. At one level, there is much to admire in Jo's holding out for perfection. Doesn't India deserve a building that stands out as an outstanding example of all that is possible when multiple disabilities are considered at the architectural level? Then again, that waiting for perfection seems impractical, oddly out of touch with reality for an organization that unflinchingly faces the travails of life with disabilities. To those close to her, including the members of the Latika Board, the building is something of a nemesis, a reminder of wishful thinking, of not being practical enough.

'I have never been anxious about money for Latika,' says Jo. One year there was a big hole in the budget with no funding in sight. Jo appealed to a well-known philanthropist. 'She didn't know me at all,' remembers Jo, 'but a cheque, for the exact amount required, showed up. It has always worked, down to the last rupee.'[262] (Another cheque followed with enough money to run Latika for a year. It came with conditions: that Jo put in systems, get professionals to track and manage data, etc.)

'When I think of all the coincidences which surround me,' says Jo. 'I cannot but think of the hand of God. It was surrendering to some other power.'[263] One of Jo and Ravi's favourite quotes from the Bible, read out at their wedding, is:

> 'Consider the lilies of the field, how they grow. They neither toil, nor spin yet I assure you, not even Solomon in all his glory was arrayed as one of these. Why then do you worry, saying, "What shall we eat?" and "What shall we drink?"'[264]

'And as to me, I know of nothing else but miracles,' wrote the American poet, Walt Whitman.[265] Remember the magnificent Latika building that wasn't getting built?

In April 2022, the phone rings. At the other end, Jo says, triumph in her voice, 'Guess a number!'[266] A big donor had fallen through, but other well-known funders, impressed by Latika's high-quality work have begun to contribute. By April 2025, 80 per cent of the building is complete. It is an incredible space, painstakingly designed with an eye to accessibility, beauty, and care.

The net, irritatingly and magically, has appeared.

11

Latika Grows Up

A start-up absorbs not just the entrepreneur but her entire family in its energy and growth. Just ask Anand and Cathleen – their childhood was punctuated by Latika's evolution.

Cathleen was eight when Latika began. She remembers there were no boundaries between work and home. 'Paula and Shaila lived right across from us and would come home in the evenings. It was great fun for me,' she says.[267] 'I was very, very involved in the evening-play programme,' recalls Anand. 'Mom couldn't find a good place for us to have creative play time. She saw enough of a need in the neighbourhood to create it. I was a direct beneficiary of that – I went every single day, made lots of friends.'[268]

In some ways, the real start of Latika was the creation of the school in 1995. 'Mom got this real sense of purpose with the school,' says Anand. 'Any neighbourhood mom could have organized the evening play-group. The school was unique.' The approach of fun, bright colours and creativity that Jo had introduced in the evening play-group was extended into the school for children with disabilities. It was a startling and joyful change. Until then, says Anand, 'there were only old-fashioned sad, Dickensian places that reeked of charity and seemed like a dumping ground for kids and adults with disabilities. From day one, the Latika school felt like a very different kind of place.'[269]

Family members chipped in. Those in the United States would send money or much needed educational toys, books and materials for the Latika school. Most of Jo's nieces and nephews from the United States have interned at Latika. Tom, Jo's brother-in-law, once dressed up as Santa Claus, much to the delight of the Latika children. 'My husband saw their monstrous computers on one of our visits, and got them three decent ones,' recalls Nutan, Ravi's sister. 'I was their brochure designer in the early years: Photoshop, desktop-design and publishing for Latika. We gave Jo the first fancy camera she had,' she says.

Funding was always in crisis. One day, in 2005, Nutan saw Jo very dismayed, worried that Latika may have to shut down. 'At that time, I had some insurance money,' says Nutan, whose husband passed away unexpectedly young, 'so I said, "Jo, have no fear, Nutan is here." And I wrote her a big cheque for $50,000.'[270] Nutan had children to raise and other obligations, but didn't think twice of giving Jo what was, at that time, almost 30 per cent of the Latika budget.[271]

Developmental paediatricians are as rare as fireflies in the night. Dr Vibha Krishnamurthy trained at Boston's Children's Hospital and returned to India to set up Ummeed, a Mumbai-based organization that helps children with special needs. Vibha is one of Latika's tribe of super-women.

Ummeed has supported Latika extensively in its growth, especially in training employees. 'Ummeed runs brilliant training programmes – everyone we have sent there has come back transformed,' says Jo. 'Our staff find the material, the way in which the training is done and how quickly they can connect what is taught there to what is done here, at Latika, so useful. Shivani, for example, came back after Ummeed's autism training and said, "Jo didi, what

Ummeed does is magic."'[272] Vibha has become one of Jo's closest friends. 'There's nothing we do not talk about. She was pivotal for Moy. Vibha also helped me in organizational growth: how to support senior staff, how to judge who is a good fit for Latika,' Jo says.[273]

In 2016, Vibha was conducting an assessment at Latika. She came across a child with autism who had not been diagnosed by Latika's screens. To ensure that such a mistake would not recur, a team called ARTists was formed; short-form for the Autism Response Team, and led by honorary Super-woman, Ajay Sharma.[274]

Ajay designed a three-day intensive-training programme, which taught the Latika team how to assess a child with autism and how to use the Autism Diagnostic Observation Schedule (ADOS), a standardized test for autism spectrum disorders. Early diagnosis is crucial, and autism can be diagnosed at under two years of age. The training happened while Ajay was in Dehradun, but much of the mentoring took place when he was back home in London. He encouraged the Latika team to prepare a written template to ensure standardization of work and a high standard of quality. 'The main difficulty [in learning] is something that is very cultural,' says Ajay. 'It's a culture of deference. They don't ask questions. As if asking questions makes you seem ignorant. Parents, because they are desperate, have better discussions. I have managed to break that barrier with some of the Latika staff.'[275]

'We set up a system: they would post a video on a private YouTube channel,' Ajay recalls. 'This would be followed by a Skype call – almost every Friday.'[276] In the calls, he would provide detailed critiques, showing the autism team how to improve. As the team gained in experience, the frequency of calls went down. The nature of the calls also changed. They went from discussions of protocols to discussions of particularly challenging cases. Soon, a pattern was established where he would work with one team after another: the autism team, the motor-disorder team, behavioural challenges, and so on. With each team Ajay would evaluate the situation, work with them on creating processes and protocols, on documentation and on evaluation. As an outsider who speaks Hindi, whose gentle manner and experience have earned him deep respect from the employees, he is perfectly positioned for providing such mentoring.

Jo thinks Ajay feels an incompleteness in Latika's current staff – the lack of doctors who specialize in developmental paediatrics.[277] The problem is not Latika-specific; India has very few. Even the United States has fewer than a thousand.[278] Jo hopes to set up a Fellowship programme that specializes in development paediatrics, with Ajay coming once a year to coach the Fellows. Ummeed, in Mumbai, came up with the idea, and Jo's replicating it. 'India's medical school system has no programme for this,' says Jo. 'So, our goal is to train for ourselves.'[279]

As children grow, so do organizations. Informal ways of hiring, training and decision-making that work well with a handful of employees need to be systematized. Feedback loops need to be created so an organization can learn and improve. It isn't easy to go from the heady days of a start-up, where everyone chips in, where you are running things by the seat of your pants, to a calm, organized place with policies, systems and well-articulated methods of operation.

Paula, Nicola, Anne, Edmund, all put in place systems in their areas of expertise – special education, child rights, therapy, photography. By 2018 though, there was no clear sense of how Latika was performing overall. It is easy, especially in a small city with no competition, to get complacent. Jo turned once again, to Ajay.

'Jo phoned me about doing a review. I said I really don't want to,' recalls Ajay. 'I have done enough, in my career.'[280] But Jo, whether it is charming a donor for funds, talking to a landlord for space, or getting someone to agree to a photograph on Latika's annual calendar, can be extremely persuasive. Soon,

Ajay found himself on his way to India to conduct a full evaluation of Latika.

'I thought there would be more obstacles of people talking [to me], especially their weaknesses or what's not working,' he says.[281] His years of mentoring Latika employees, however, had built up a rapport and trust; the work went smoothly. 'The willingness of the team to learn and listen deserves credit too. They are really humble and open,' adds Jo.[282] Having agreed, Ajay was very thorough. Over three weeks he spent time in every centre and spoke to all the main groups – parents, children, employees, coordinators, etc. He observed not just the therapists and educators in action, but also how new parents are greeted at the gate or how the drivers treat the children on the school-run. He made his way through dusty files, and created detailed surveys in Hindi and English. The review was conducted with 'a kind of rigour we have never experienced in an evaluation before,' says Jo.[283]

What emerges resoundingly from the report is how much both parents and staff value Latika. Parents trust the Latika employees with their children, have a comforting sense of safety, and appreciate what they learn to do with their child.

The employees in turn, appreciate the strong culture of mutual respect and feel supported by Latika. There are of course, areas for improvement.

Parents would like more 'time per day given to children ... better availability of speech therapists and... access to an occupational therapist.' Parents also crave 'more training about how best to support their child at home.' The employees, meanwhile, would like 'the systems and processes to improve to better support their work.'[284]

By the early 2000s Latika was established. Its early diagnosis centre, services of physiotherapy, special education and home plans were functioning well. Shubha Nagesh was sifting through data when she stumbled across something disturbing. 'I realized many girls were dropping out after Latika's first assessments,' Shubha says. Sebastian Gruschke (who is fluent in Hindi) and she decided to investigate. They visited families within the city and faraway. Why were parents not bringing their girls in regularly?

'One girl was lying in bed, staring at the fan all day,' recalls Shubha.[285] A UNICEF report, while focusing on what has improved for girls around the world since 1995, states, 'Today, discrimination and limiting stereotypes remain rife.'[286] If money is limited, the boy gets the education, more nutritious food and access to healthcare. The impact of such disparities is magnified with a disability. In India, the illiteracy rate for males with disabilities is 43 per cent; for women with disabilities, it rises to a shocking 64 per cent.[287]

Thanks to Latika's outreach programme (which sends a roving team of specialists to seek families with disabilities in areas outside the city), the bedridden girl now comes to Latika regularly. She's able to move around, take in the colours, the play, the world around her. Another girl was kept locked up at home. Not out of malice but out of fear because she has Down syndrome, and had reached menarche. 'We worked with the mother to overcome her fears,' says Shubha. 'To understand her daughter's need for social interaction. Can the girl manage menstruation on her own? Can she learn to wear a pad, can she dispose of it on her own?'[288] Through Latika, the mothers met each other, learned as a group. Latika created a messaging service and short videos to provide much needed support, to help address their fears. Now, more than 400 girls with a range of disabilities benefit from this service.

Inevitably, an organization experiences setbacks as it grows. Experienced people leave, beloved projects falter, what works well in small groups fails with expansion. At Latika, the setbacks were in the flagship centre, the partnership with the government, and in a drop in long-term, highly-skilled volunteers.

With Sebastian Gruschke, Gubbara, the assessment centre, flourished at the government-run Doon Hospital. As a doctor Sebastian was able to coordinate with government doctors in the same building. As a foreigner, he won hearts by speaking Hindi and even writing his assessment reports in Hindi. When he moved back to the Netherlands, Gubbara was still at Doon Hospital, serving hundreds of babies. However, the colourful Gubbara centre with its friendly, welcoming staff, became too much of a contrast to the rest of the public hospital. It showed the hospital staff all that they might have wanted to provide but couldn't. All that they might want to be, but were not. Tensions rose as doctors would delay reports or examinations. Trouble arose between Latika employees and those working for Doon Hospital. The public-private partnership broke down.

Gubbara bumped along in other buildings, before coming to rest with the other centres at the main Latika building. The price was paid by children and parents. Numbers receiving care fell sharply. An evaluation in 2019 found that 'The assessments and follow-ups of high-risk neonates ... have almost ceased ... referrals have declined ... mainly due to the impact of these relocations.'[289]

Jo has come to view this part of Latika's history as less of an experience that leaves a bitter taste in the mouth, and more as something that had some influence on national policy. The collaboration attracted a lot of attention – government officials from across the country came to see the model at work. In the seven years that Gubbara was at Doon Hospital, the visitors included the Health Secretary, Government of India, the Health Secretary, Punjab, the former Deputy Director of the National Institute of Mental Health and many others.

Poonam Natarajan, Chairperson, National Trust from the Ministry of Social Justice and Empowerment, Government of India, visited in 2013 and wrote, 'At last I have achieved what I have been waiting to do for a long time – visit Gubbara. A fabulous facility to meet a vital need in our country for early intervention. Many congratulations. I do hope the National Trust can help replicate this model.' Pranajyoti Nath, a senior IAS officer all the way from Kerala, visited and wrote, 'It is a brilliant experience. This needs to be replicated in every state hospital in the country.' By May 2014, a national programme was rolled out, setting up District EICs across the country.

In its first decade and a half, Latika had a number of highly skilled professionals with decades of experience, coming from Europe and the United

States, generously giving their time and expertise. There was Paula Hughes, the special educator who came as a VSO volunteer for a summer and stayed twelve years, Anne Bruce, the speech and hearing therapist from NHS Scotland who had multiple visits over a decade, Edmund Cluett, who taught Jo photography, a skill that eloquently captures the joy that lies at the heart of Latika, Nicola Tansley, the educational psychologist who instilled child rights, Sebastian Gruschke, the doctor at Latika for five years and who helped set up the assessment and EIC. There were also other skilled foreign and Indian volunteers who would come in the summers and winters – bringing in new ideas, a breath of fresh air, into the rapidly growing organization. 'It was the presence of these people with their first-rate skills and unusual ability who helped Latika grow,' says Jo's husband, Ravi. 'People coming from faraway cities like Chandigarh and Lucknow would say, "We have not seen a place like this." It was amazing to see Jo develop at the same time. She was a college dropout activist. And here she is running such a large institution!'[290]

Dunu Roy who used to visit regularly in the early years, is concerned about a drop in the very inputs that nurtured Latika. 'International and national inputs – that's slacked off,' he says.[291] Some decline in long-term volunteers is natural. Nicola Tansey and Anne Bruce, for instance, have grown too old to make the journey. Speaking on the sunlit balcony of the Latika office, Ajay Sharma says, 'My role has changed. Only if the teams have an issue, they turn to me. It is a big shift that has happened, as it should be.'[292] It is a natural evolution as a fledgling organization, grows and becomes self-assured in its functioning. 'We have research projects with Nimhans and Ummeed, interns from the US, Australia and England, Teach for India Fellows visiting to learn our approach, and lots of other technical partnerships,' says Jo. Ravi points out that the nature of interaction has changed: 'Earlier, it was international experts coming here. Now, it is Latika on the international stage.'[293]

When should a leader step down? In the private sector, the Starbucks founder Howard Shultz, for example, has returned as CEO multiple times. It is just as challenging in non-profits.

Some of the difficulty stems from a founder's attachment. The organization is their baby, they have put in the hard work. To cut the umbilical cord is harrowing. Leaving raises searing, existential questions: 'Who am I if not the founder of this organization?'

The external world feeds that emphasis. The founder is the face of the organization. Donors and conference organizers insist on meeting or inviting only her. Nobody else is given the same importance, no matter how much the founder might try otherwise. Board members, who have championed the founder, have to start afresh with a new, unknown CEO. Staff members who have followed the founder through many battles may resist a change in leadership. Research done by Monitor-Deloitte, an international consulting company, found that 'Outgoing founders are either focusing their emotional energy on their next big step or retiring and leaving their life's work in the hands of a relative stranger ... It's an environment that is inescapably fraught with very real human emotions that have the potential to significantly disrupt or stall an organization's development.'[294]

'Founders find it very hard to let go,' remarks Ritu Arora Jain, former Latika Board member and now coach to Jo Chopra. 'They can be insensitive when the CEO they have hired wants to do more.'[295] These challenges are not unique to Jo and Latika. 'I have seen it over and over again,' says Ritu.

Passion, hard work and energy are poured into the founding of an organization. The entrepreneur doesn't see boundaries between family and work, often actively dissolving such divisions. This was certainly true at Latika. Moy Moy's needs were met by the creation of Latika, which went on to serve hundreds of children like her. Moy's helpers moved from home to office, to become the core team at Latika. Jo's older children, Anand and Cathleen, and husband, Ravi, participated in brain-storming sessions, hosting Jo's colleagues, and generally helping out wherever needed.

The early days were heady; all dreams were possible. Jo juggled many duties – providing high-quality care to children with special needs, finding and training employees, bringing in the funds, increasing the scope of what Latika does, raising her own children (including tackling Moy's increasing disabilities), looking after her in-laws and other relatives, being a good friend to a vast network, and much more. Then, blink, and twenty-five years have gone by.

There are the changing needs of the organization to consider. A founder may be perfect for the initial years – to surmount staggering challenges, magic-up resources where none exist, inspire the team to work doggedly, not for money but for a shared dream. A decade or two in, though, the organization needs something else, someone else. Its employee base has grown, services provided multiplied. Decisions that were made on the fly or through individual conversations now need to be documented. Processes are required, as are good management and efficient systems. None of these may be the core strengths of the founder.

Much of this is true for Jo and Latika. The flip side of passion, joy and high energy, is a disinclination for what can be seen as the boring stuff – putting in systems. A board member did a SWOT analysis. A long-time volunteer pointed out the need for management rigour. Jo would agree to their feedback. As a voracious reader, she'd devour recommended books like Joan Magretta's *What Management Is*, or John Doerr's *Measure What Matters.* She tried to put into place a measuring system like OKRs (Objectives and Key Results) that Doerr recommends for goal-setting. But as an activist, a maverick, a woman who has always boldly carved her own way, going from big picture to detailed processes is a challenge. So even if other staff members eagerly take to OKRs, the project failed without demonstration from the top. Her sharp mind sees the need for systems, it is the follow-through that falls apart. 'It is a failure, I see it,' Jo says with complete openness. 'She didn't believe in systems, formal stuff!' echoes her husband, Ravi.[296]

Google's founders brought in Eric Schmidt to stabilize their start-up. Mark Zuckerberg brought in Sheryl Sandberg at Facebook. Latika's need for systems saw three Chief Operating Officers (COO) come and go, before an in-house solution worked. Sumita Nanda, the current COO, has a relationship with all the employees, has worked up the ranks of the organization, and knows Latika intimately. 'What Jo did is sensible,' remarks Ravi. 'Sumita runs the organization on a day-to-day basis. She comes to Jo when it is a grave issue.'[297] The issue of who will take over from Jo, though, remains. Ritu Arora Jain puts it well. 'It needs maturity and understanding on both sides,' she says. 'The founder is saying, 'Take this off my plate, but interfere minimally in the areas that I am good at and want to keep.' The new person might be joining with a passion to do it all, not just the five things you want him to do.'[298]

Ritu herself has moved from the corporate world to the non-profit one, so she sees the lacunae on both sides. Those with decades of work experience in the private sector are trained to be critical, to analyse issues and then try and fix them immediately. 'They don't know to pause and see, "Why is it working or not working?" "What can I learn?"' she remarks. 'Things are done for a reason [in this non-profit]. Can you learn before changing things in a massive way?' The newcomer has to practice patience, something that's difficult to do when you have, for years, worked towards a quick demonstration of your worth.'

'With enormous sympathy for both sides,' Ritu adds, 'The founder should not feel threatened. The board members should support both people. The organization should let the new CEO have some quick wins. It is not easy for an external person: he or she is stepping into an organization where every staff member has been groomed by the founder for the past fifteen or more years. The person from outside has to continuously prove himself to the rest of the organization, who may view him with skepticism or even suspicion.'[299]

'I think that Jo has begun to step back a little,' says Ravi. He's in their living room, with Jo and close friends, talking about the future of Latika. 'You have taken time off to reflect on what all you do,' Ravi says, addressing Jo. 'You have brought in competent managers who are taking on a lot of your worries on the operational front. Now, you should concentrate on the ethos part: how Latika looks upon the children, the idea of a more caring world – that is your unique contribution.'[300]

12

The Effect of a Virus

Everybody has a pandemic story. Latika's started with a critical question: When you have placed face-to-face contact at the centre of your model, how do you reach your children and families in a pandemic?

Time has eased our memories: the fearful uncertainty of the early months, the long lines and empty shelves in the supermarket, the shudder at the sound of a hollow cough. Sanitize hands, put on a mask, wipe down surfaces; the added routines felt endless. Lockdown in India was fierce, imposed practically overnight. Millions of migrant workers were forced to walk away from their daily wages, bags on head and shoulders, trying desperately to catch any bus or train that would get them closer to home.

The waves of the pandemic were unrelenting. By 2021, more than 500,000 Indians had died of the virus.[301] The rich, normally sheltered by their wealth, were queuing up outside hospitals, pleading for beds. Stories abounded of people dying in their cars from lack of oxygen, of families saying their farewells on video, of bodies being buried or cremated with no ritualistic goodbyes.

A national crisis, a war, or an epidemic often amplifies existing inequalities. A scramble for resources (in this case masks, hospital beds, oxygen and vaccination), puts immense stress on an already creaking public health system. Families see expenditures mount while income shrivels. Inevitably, the most vulnerable suffer disproportionately. For example, 60 per cent of the deaths attributed to COVID-19 in the United Kingdom were among the disabled.[302]

In a pandemic, several questions arise for a society at large, all accentuated for those with disabilities: how are those with disabilities living? Are they dependent on a caregiver who was coming in daily? Is there a higher rate of co-morbidities that will have an impact on a COVID-19 infection? How do you isolate if you live in dense neighbourhoods and have physical, mental or other conditions? Like a delicate spider's web, families with special-needs children create a carefully balanced, finely crafted social network of care. A single stroke, like isolation forced by lockdown, sweeps that web away. How do you explain to a boy with severe autism that masks need to be kept on, to a girl with Down syndrome that you cannot hug those you used to hug before, to a teenager with cerebral palsy, in a wheelchair, that his one bright spark in the day, of meeting his friends at school, has been snuffed out?

'Many parents did not have internet on their phones. Some didn't even have phones. Some had migrated,' recalls Shubha, who led Latika's outreach services. How would the children, who learnt so much from their in-person special school and therapy sessions, be able to manage at home? Would there be delays in their development? How would the educators and therapists assess and assist by peering at small screens? Adapting to the pandemic was more than merely a matter of access to wi-fi. There was no time for training, mapping or planning. What happened at Latika was a *tour de force*.

The early days of the pandemic were marked by misinformation and confusion. Latika countered this by sorting through global and domestic medical recommendations from reliable sources, and sharing information on the virus, how it spreads, the different ways in which one could try and avoid infection. 'Dr Shubha and Jo didi [who was stuck in the United States], really guided us so well,' says Manju Subedi. Everything was translated into the local language. This was done not once but at regular intervals, squashing rumours that trended viciously across social media. Employees were assured that they and their families, if affected, would be supported.[303] They in turn had to figure out how to pass this information and assurance to the Latika families. After twenty-five years of working in-person, Latika embraced technology and new ways of doing things. 'In ten days of planning in lockdown we started online classes. We made plans for the staff. We were calling each and every child. Very poor families who did not have mobile phones were given phones by Latika,' says Manju.[304]

The Latika employees, while struggling with the effects of the pandemic in their own homes, used every form of technology to communicate. Community aides with boundless patience worked their way through hundreds of phone numbers, calling parents to offer support. Centre heads used WhatsApp messages to keep in touch with their teams and monitor progress. The psychologist checked up not just on the children but also on their parents, gently testing for mental-health issues.

In lockdown, parents were encouraged to send videos of their child so therapists could see how exercises were being done and then follow-up with modifications. Some Latika staff members innovatively used their own children as models to demonstrate an activity. Mothers, who are often the main caregivers, were frazzled by having their children, their spouse and their in-laws all at home, all day. Latika urged families to develop a routine for the children, as though they were in school – reading, helping in household chores, exercises, engagement. The parent could always pick up the phone and call.[305] 'At home we were told, "You are only doing Latika work – pay some attention to the house and your own child, please,"' says Manju Subedi with a smile. 'Before COVID-19, work was from 8 a.m. to 4 p.m. In lockdown, it was full time. 11 p.m., I was getting calls. Is it a child? Is it a staff member? What do I do? I have to pick up the phone.'[306]

As the pressures on the families mounted, especially on those with limited resources, Latika stepped in some more. Employees made bundles of books, toys and disability-specific products and distributed them. 'We started medical and food support,' recalls Manju. 'Sumita didi and a driver bhaiya would, in those very risky times, go home-to-home to help. It was fantastic.'[307] Kits of oxygen cylinders, pulse-oximeters and masks were created, to be shared wherever possible. The Resource Centre team at Latika tried to stay on top of the latest, evidence-based COVID-19 information, translate it, and share it with all Latika employees, parents and children. It had to be simple, easy to understand and follow in order to tamp down fear and prevent the virus spreading.

India had one of the world's largest vaccination roll-outs.[308] Over the course of the pandemic more than 950 million individuals were vaccinated.[309] For Latika families who live cheek-by-jowl, social distancing was not just impossible, it seemed like a cruel joke. So, vaccination was one solution. Here too, Latika waded in, determined to be safe. There are many reasons why someone with a disability may not get vaccinated. If the vaccinations are being given in a building with steps but no wheelchair ramp, then they cannot reach the centre. If the centre is crowded with lots of people pushing to get through, it makes it challenging to navigate. If there are bright lights and loud noises, children with behavioural issues might act out.[310]

Rizwan Ali, Latika's one-man legal army, fought tooth-and-nail for government approval to organize a Latika-specific vaccination camp, so that employees, parents and older children could be vaccinated in a safe, well-organized manner, surrounded by familiar, kind, smiling faces. 'There was so much solidarity,' Shubha recalls. 'We came together, Latika as an organization and all the families who use us.'[311]

The families, even those who were just beginning a relationship with Latika, quickly realized one thing: Latika was the *only* life-line for them. 'In the house, in the pandemic, everything was done for the child,' says Neelam Rawat, a Latika parent.[312] 'Everything else was closed down,' Shubha remembers. 'Private centres, other organizations, government services, everything.'[313]

At a time when big companies with deep pockets were cutting jobs, Latika went out of its way to prevent such a thing. 'All senior staff took a thirty percent cut in salary,' says Sumita. 'We did not touch the salaries of those who earned less than Rs 20,000. We wrote to our donors asking for extensions ... We had hired a helper [at the bottom of the office hierarchy], a week before lockdown, but we did not fire him.'[314] Not a single person at Latika was laid off.

13

Where Do We Go from Here?

Your absence has gone through me
Like thread through a needle.
Everything I do is stitched with its colour.

from 'Separation' by W.S. Merwin[315]

The phone rings. Jo and Cathleen are in windy Chicago, sipping coffee, chatting casually, intimately, as mothers and daughters do. Jo steps outside the café to hear clearly. It's Ravi, from their home in India. Moy Moy's been ill, so he has been calling twice a day. The doctor had just come by and Moy was better, Ravi said. 'I'm going to take the phone to Moy Moy, perhaps she will make a noise. Or you can at least hear her breathing.' Ravi goes in to the bedroom with the phone, and then, he says, 'Jo, Moy Moy's gone. She's gone.'[316]

One of Jo's cherished Christian verses is, 'The eternal God is your dwelling place, and underneath are the everlasting arms.'[317] The peace that single line offers did not come through in July 2018. How could it? Our religions talk about death. We know it comes to every one of us. Yet, optimistically, we believe that those we love will be with us forever.

Even though Ravi knew Moy Moy had died at home, he took her to the hospital driven by that last desperate hope that she could be revived. It's the monsoon season and absolutely pouring down. At 11 p.m., Ravi returns home, heart-broken. Slowly, quietly, the women show up, one-by-one, to help – Moy Moy's caregivers from over the years. None of them owns a car. They come on rickety motor-cycles or auto-rickshaws in the dark, on slippery roads, getting drenched to the bone.

Death in India is like life on its streets, up close and personal, with no sanitized distance. All arrangements have to be put together by those who are grieving. So, Moy Moy's body is at home, not in a funeral parlour. The group of caregivers send their husbands out to buy big blocks of ice to preserve Moy's body. 'These women are some of my closest friends,' says Jo. 'I couldn't imagine my life without them. They don't speak English, they don't have fancy degrees, they don't have great educations ... but when we needed them, they were there. When Moy Moy needed them, they were there.'[318] These women prepare Moy's body, rearrange the living room, and stay with the body. They stay that night, the next day and the following night, until Jo, Cathleen and Anand are able to scramble on flights from the United States and England and come home.

'How can you abandon us?' rails Shivani. We are sitting on the carpeted floor of a small therapy room at Latika. 'Moy Moy comes to me in my dreams, often. I talk to her.'[319]

There is not a speck of doubt in Shivani's mind that Moy was the beating heart of Latika. 'Look at my life. How many people I have met, how much I have changed. All because of Moy,' she says. '*Woh kitne logon ke ghar ke chule jalati hai.* ("How many home-fires burn because of Moy.")[320]

Shivani has risen through the ranks at Latika to become a senior special educator. Being with Latika from the early days onwards means that she was with Moy Moy for years. 'I don't know if Moy was a daughter or sister,' she says. 'Her loss was like losing a physical limb.'[321]

Moy at twenty-nine, was at Latika till the very end. She came to school two days before she died. She was at the All-Staff Meeting, in her usual position, up-front, in her special wheelchair.

'When I really miss Moy, I smell some of her stuff,' Shivani says. She is weeping, struggling to talk as memories flood in. 'Jo didi gave me her scarf, her funnel, and it still smells of her. '*Mera manna hai, ke Moy hamare dil aur dimag mein hai*', ('I truly believe that Moy is in our hearts and minds'), Shivani says. '*Main acchhe din ko yaad karti hu.*' ('I remember the good days'), when she demanded things, when she laughed.'[322]

Shivani thinks the spirit of Latika will continue without Moy, but only if the organization manages to keep its heart alive. 'We need to increase our skills but not say, "I won't do this, I won't do that,"' she says. 'If we can keep the good things alive, the new staff members will learn from us.' And what are those good things? She looks up through her just-dried tears, and gives her characteristic smile that lights up the room, 'Our attitude and our giving nature.'[323]

'Buttercup!' exclaims Ravi, looking at a photograph of Moy Moy dressed in bright yellow. Of the two, Jo is the talker, the discusser. She has an enormous global network of family and friends. Ravi is quieter, opening up occasionally with unexpectedly funny stories and memories. Jo wrote about her struggles and sought a therapist's professional assistance after Moy died. With Ravi, it is harder to know how he came to terms with his daughter's death. A glimpse of his deep love and tenderness are seen at Moy Moy's memorial service in New Hampshire:

> 'I don't know if you believe in angels?' Ravi asks the audience.
>
> 'I certainly didn't, but this kid over here (pointing to Moy's photograph) transformed that thinking.
>
> I'd like to remember her like the photo – full of mischief. She was an angel who came to us. Her arrival was totally unexpected and unplanned. She was not born to us, that's why I say "she came to us" ... After some death-defying odds, she came to us – barely two weeks old, weighing less than a kilogram. In her early days, when she was knee-high, she was always full of humour and pranks.
>
> 'She spoke our human language for a while (remember, she's an angel), in her own stilted way and then laughed. Laughter was her real language. She thought our human language was a strange way to communicate. We tried to teach her the alphabet, but she laughed that away too! She knew it would be of no use to her.

'We sent her to school with her siblings, Cathleen and Anand. She tried that for a little while, but then let us know that "it's not for me." She needed a special school for herself and many friends, and this need her mother, Jo, understood very well.

'By the time she was eight or nine, she settled down to fulfil her mission. She became quiet. Human language was going to be of little use to her. From then on, she spoke with her eyes and her smile. And she accomplished a tremendous mission.

She is gone now. (Ravi breaks down here, crying.) Her task is done with us. Her departure was just as swift and unexpected as her arrival ... but I am sure she has alighted somewhere else on Earth, and she has found a new home to accomplish a new mission.'[324]

The *Brahma Kamal* is the state flower of Uttarakhand where Latika is. In Hinduism, the flower is considered sacred, symbolizing purity and divinity. Lord Bramha, the creator, is said to have shaped it in his form. It blooms only at night, and only for twelve hours. A bit like Moy Moy, magically here, and then, gone.

How long does it take for a parent to come to terms with the grief of losing a child? How long for a sibling? It is December 2020. The pandemic is raging, so Moy Moy's second memorial service is hosted online. Cathleen remembers how after Moy's funeral people had gathered at home. A neighbour, having expressed his condolences, was heading out. He turned casually at the door, and asks her an unanswerable question: '*Tumhare bachpan ki saheli chali gayi, ab tum kya karoge?*' ('Your childhood companion has gone away, what will you do now?')

Parents are supposed to die before their children in the natural scheme of things. How does one navigate such a loss? Is there a date, a deadline, for life to return to 'normal'? There are the 'firsts' – the first birthday, Diwali, Thanksgiving and Christmas without Moy Moy. There is the giving away of her clothes (and seeing the shirts, dresses and shoes on a number of children in the neighbourhood, bright, unexpected reminders in the most routine of places). The rugged stroller that was Moy's chariot, in which Jo took her everywhere, still sits on the porch, getting a little dusty. For Jo, work at Latika was so closely tied with Moy Moy. One was because the other was.

'Since she died, I have been quite blank,' says Jo. 'I need something and haven't found it yet.' Her faith provides some strength and comfort. 'I've left the Catholic Church but I haven't given up its teachings,'

Jo writes. 'I still believe in an afterlife, I think. I still believe in the existence of a soul that outlives the physical body. I believe it because I feel Moy Moy's presence everywhere, in my waking and sleeping; in the hearts and minds of those who knew her and, mysteriously, at work in the lives of people who've never met her and have never even heard of her.'[325]

Moy is buried in a beautiful cemetery. It is on the way to the airport. 'I have this ritual whenever I am leaving town,' says Jo, 'I stop off and say, "Hi."'[329]

Jo is a big believer in miracles. On the first anniversary of Moy Moy's death, Ravi and Jo were at their daughter Cathleen's apartment in Chicago. 'We woke up feeling tender and fragile, wondering how we would get through this sad, painful day,' remembers Jo.[326] 'I opened my email after breakfast and found the news of a donation of $150,000. The donor had never met Moy, didn't know me, and had no idea of the significance of receiving this stunning amount on this particular day. The atmosphere lightened immediately – like Moy Moy was laughing and saying: "What? You thought I was gone?"'[327]

That day, Jo was keen to return to the spot where she had taken Ravi's phone call from India, telling her their world had changed forever, that Moy Moy had just died. They get there and it looks ... different. 'I don't remember it like this,' Jo remarks. Cathleen replies, 'I know Mom, they changed this whole thing

– made a Zen stone garden, and a bench – just to sit there and reflect, on that spot.'[328]

'Moy was such a force,' says Mamta Govil. 'What strikes you is the complete cover of love that surrounded all of them. It was almost unreal.'[329] Moy Moy defied the odds. Despite increasing disabilities as she grew older, she triumphed through severe illnesses including typhoid and pneumonia, and had chronic seizures. She went from a funny, mobile, verbal child (at four, with cognitive delay and cerebral palsy, when asked if she's ready to go to church, Moy would raise both arms over her head and holler, 'Hallowed be thy name!') to one who gradually lost all those traits.

When she was five years old, speech stopped. Every night, as she was put to bed, after a loving prayer said with her mum, Moy would reply, 'Goodnight! Love you.' That whittled down to: 'love you,' and then, silence. When you pause to consider it – "Love you" – seems like the perfect phrase with which to gracefully bow out of the speaking world.

By the time she hit double-digits, she was non-speaking and, in a wheelchair. In her teens her inability to swallow meant living with a feeding tube inserted directly into her stomach. There was nothing she could do for herself.

And yet, and yet and yet ... there were so many benefits from her life. At the memorial for Moy,

Ravi said, 'We were lucky beyond belief. Moy Moy constantly reminded us never to dismiss anyone as unable to accomplish the amazing. She saw the light in everyone she met and she encouraged them to use that light to make this world a kinder, more loving place.'[330]

A year later, at the memorial in New Hampshire, Jo echoed his words: 'Moy Moy left us with what I call the disabled mind (and I mean that with the greatest possible respect and love). With a disabled mind you do not make any assumptions. She taught us that everybody is capable of something, everybody has a gift, everybody is precious. If Moy Moy could do it – she couldn't walk, couldn't talk, couldn't even swallow, and yet look at what she accomplished. That gives us hope that we all have some great gift to give to the world.'[331]

'I have a slight anxiety about such things,' says Ajay. 'That often such people can become icons.' We are discussing how Latika will carry on after the death of Moy Moy. Latika was started for Moy. It grew around her and her growing needs. Jo took Moy Moy everywhere. Moy had the starring role in Latika's beautiful, much awaited annual calendar. What happens to an organization when its poster-child passes away? 'What do you say to a person? Everything sounds superficial or trite, yeah?' asks Ajay.[332] He sent Jo a stirringly beautiful poem by Emily Dickinson, 'We Grow Accustomed to the Dark,' after Moy's death. He reads it out, peering at his mobile phone screen. It has everything in it. It acknowledges the darkness, the bleakness but also how, afterwards, life lights up again.

Vibha Krishnamurthy, in Mumbai, brushes away the notion of Moy Moy being the heart of Latika. We are speaking on the phone, both stuck at home in what is one of the fiercest coronavirus lockdowns in the world. Vibha knows Jo very well, calls Jo her 'BFF.' As founders of organizations that work with children with disabilities, Vibha and Jo are often invited speakers at the same conferences, meeting in different cities all across the country.

'You know, that might be true in Dehradun. But I have known Jo outside Dehradun, have seen Latika through her eyes. Jo has grieved, but she continues [to carry on]. The organization culture will remain,' says Vibha. Then she adds insightfully, 'I think it is not Moy Moy but *Jo* who is the heart of Latika. She is the one who brings the ethos of openness, joy, fun, inclusion to Latika.'[333]

It is June 2019. A large hall is packed with Latika employees gathered for the annual All-Staff Meeting – drivers, helpers, therapists, educators, they are all there. It is the first meeting without Moy Moy. She would have been seated in her stroller, in the first row. In that very spot, instead, is a lovely oil painting of Moy in cream and rust. Plastic candles flicker realistically on its base. At one point, everyone is looking at the antics on the stage and laughing. Jo's face is in profile. She turns to her right and looks at the portrait. Her face collapses in such incredible anguish. It is a sliver of a moment. There and then gone, buried somewhere deep within. In an instant, Jo is back to cheering her colleagues on, being the supportive energy of Latika.

Mamta Govil admires Jo's emergence after the death of Moy. 'Moy's passing has got Latika out in its own right,' she says. 'Jo handled it very beautifully. She's been talking to a therapist, to coaches, about handing over the reins to someone else. She is making future plans for Latika.'[334]

'We have all known the long loneliness,' wrote Dorothy Day, the famous Catholic writer and social activist, 'and we have learned that the only solution is love and that love comes with community.'[335] The community that Latika responds to – children, parents, caregivers – is alive and active and in need of help. It gives purpose to the organization, to the core team members and to the founder, who struggle with the loss of Moy's presence.

'I would like to help more in the next phase,' says Anand, Jo and Ravi's son, 'from a legacy and sustainability perspective.' At the same time, he is wary of Latika being run by the 'founding family.' 'Moy was a driving, galvanizing force,' he says, 'but actually, the long-term sustainability is going to come from the fact that Latika can show track records of dozens and dozens of children.'[336]

Jo has tussled with belonging to the Church and being liberal, for years. In the 2000s, an enormous scandal shook the Church. Award-winning investigative reporting by the *Boston Globe* broke the story that hundreds of priests had abused children in their spiritual care. Devastatingly, the Church authorities had known and done nothing, often merely transferring the priests from one church to another.[337]

'The other big moment is when Moy Moy died,' Jo says. While Jo hadn't been to church in a long time, she turned to its familiar ritual for comfort. Cathleen organized Mass at the church in Dehradun. The place was packed: Latika employees, family and friends, well-wishers, neighbours. The priest however, did not know the family or Moy Moy. 'So,

I wrote him a big note all about Moy Moy. Cathleen and Shaila went to meet him, to explain that most of those attending Mass would not be Catholic, he should speak in Hindi, etc.' The priest didn't make the time to meet them and so they left the note for him.

At the funeral, the priest got up to give the homily. To the horror of Ravi, Jo, Anand, Cathleen and others who knew Moy so well, it rapidly became clear that the priest had not read the note. 'He spoke in English. He didn't know *anything* about her other than she was disabled,' remembers Jo. 'He went on and on about how deprived she was, how thankful we should be to God that we are normal.'

The priest, following Church law, would only give communion to the Catholics in the audience. Cathleen, just as fed up as Jo, on a day when they were reeling from the loss of Moy, while trying to celebrate her life, had had enough. She walked up to the priest and said, 'Father, if everyone here can't take communion, no one will.'[338]

'Certainly, all the Catholics that I hung out [with] would be horrified by his behaviour,' says Jo. 'It was just one more thing that made me stop.'[339]

Again, though, faith showed up in a different way. Moy's body was taken to Latika. The staff had quietly closed the organization for two days, as a mark of respect and love. They had beautifully decorated the entire building. Slowly, mourners gathered – children and parents from Latika, alumni, well-wishers from all corners of the country. There must have been 400 or 500 people there, Jo reckons, gathered to pay their respects and to support Jo and Ravi. 'Moy is the invisible thread that calls us all home and binds us all together,' says Ravi.[340]

It isn't just the loss of Moy Moy that is changing Latika. It is also Jo's need to find a successor. Like all founder-led organizations, everyone sees the danger of Jo being too central to Latika's existence; how everything depends on her, especially the fundraising. 'I have thought about it so much,' says Aarti Nair. Aarti was an active part of the early years at Latika, first as a physiotherapist, then as head of the EIC. 'Sumita and I discuss it. I look at how Ravi has made his organization independent of him,' Aarti says.[341]

Jo goes away for long stretches of time to the United States, leaving other people in charge. During the pandemic, Jo went to the United States for the birth of her first grandchild. A three-month trip ended up lasting sixteen months, as the pandemic tore through first the United States and then India. A rotation of leadership gives senior employees an opportunity to test the CEO-position, and it gives Jo (while remaining in close contact), the chance to see how they are performing in the role. Sooner or later, a transition at Latika will have to take place.

'There's a feeling that it's a top-heavy NGO,' remarks Mamta Govil, delicately. 'The number of children has not increased in proportion. So, for that extra money spent, how much impact are you getting?' Then, with insight borne of a deep knowledge of the founder and the organization, Mamta adds, 'A strong love for Jo doesn't let us ask those questions. Not that she won't allow it, but because we think it's her way of doing it.'[342]

Some things are changing: Jo has hired a full-time person for fund-raising. She's training her colleagues in how to recognize the beautiful stories that already exist at Latika and how to use them as examples with visitors and donors.

Sebastian Gruschke feels Latika could offer more medical diagnosis and support to the parents. In his time at the organization, he felt there was a clear de-medicalization that took place. 'A child with a disability has difficulties in all domains of his or her functioning – education, learning, medical,' he explains. 'My role at Latika was of integrating the medical issues in this whole process – parents, teachers, therapists, doctors and the medical system.'[343]

There's a delicate balance in the issue Sebastian raises: how much medicalization is too much? It is easy to write prescriptions instead of giving parents non-invasive and more time-involved methods of helping a child with a disability. The flip side, however, is that parents feel they have to go to doctors on their own, without Latika support, and make their own medical decisions. Sebastian feels Latika could do with caring doctors within the organization who understand the parents, rather than the external medical system, which tends to be dismissive, especially of poor families.

A doctor can catch issues that the parents may not even know need attention. He gives the example of cerebral palsy, where children have vision and hip problems. 'The children are difficult to examine. Thus, vision problems can be misinterpreted as cognitive problems, because the child does not understand what they see. For the hips, you do x-rays to check the hip position. This is important because at an older age there may be pain and the child stops walking.'[344] Having a caring doctor who is on Latika's rolls will address the need to look out for things like this. 'The challenge,' says Jo, 'is to find a good doctor open to the entire holistic approach.'[345]

Dunu Roy, a former board member, jokes that he's no longer active at Latika because, 'I ask nasty questions from time to time.'[351] Part of his questioning is to push the organization not to rest on its laurels but to experiment and grow, whether in pedagogy or work culture. Dunu, one of Latika's oldest supporters, and Megha Girdhar, a much younger former employee, agree on one thing. As Megha puts it, 'There [need] to be more young people.' With an organization that has 'more senior folks, the young ones are not listened to. 'This is how we have always done it' – I can see it creeping in.'[346]

Dunu is quick to point out the strengths of Latika that light the road ahead: the EIC influencing state and national policy, for example. 'The earlier you catch [the disability] the sooner the parents learn and deal with it. Children also learn how to deal with the world.' And now, Latika is, 'doing a lot on advocacy, data-based, evidence-based, policy.'[347]

If you can't find the skills, hone them locally. Jo has done this exceptionally well. As Latika grew up, those in it did so too. There is a core group of women who came when they were just eighteen or nineteen years old. Twenty-five years later, they hold specialized degrees, senior positions and earn more than their eighteen-year-old selves could ever have dreamt of.

Manju Subedi is one such woman. 'I was so scared (when I first joined). Now I see that we are scared of what we do not know,' she says. 'I would wonder why to do these things [the therapy, the teaching], so slowly, like Paula said. Why not just yell at the kid?' she says, laughing at her younger self. 'Now I am trained and know the difference and the "why" of what we are doing. Qualifications matter but what really matters is experience.' Then, turning solemn, Manju, who now confidently heads the Latika school, says, 'Even I do not know how much I know. It is only after I have spoken and reacted in a good way to emotional parents, then afterwards, I look back at that interaction and say, 'Oh Manju, well-done.'[348]

Latika has gone through its storms. The passing away of its poster child, Uma (Moy Moy) Chopra-McGowan was shattering. Yet, in times of deep sorrow come unexpected bits of joy. Moy died in July 2018. That same year, in Moy Moy's birth-month of November, Hema, one of the most energetic stalwarts of Latika welcomed a new member into her family, a beautiful baby girl. They named her... Moy. '*Moy ka naam badi baat hain*,' says Hema. ('It is a big deal to be named after the original Moy.')[349]

In April 2020, in the raging COVID-19 pandemic, with more than 2.7 million people infected world-wide, and 870,000 confirmed cases in the United States,[350] Jo and Ravi's middle child, Cathleen, gave birth to a baby girl in Chicago. Her husband, Daniel, and she name her Uma.

Moy Moy met many famous people in her life: the Vice-President of India, Pope John Paul II and His Holiness the Dalai Lama. What her life showed, though, is not a path to the famous, but a focus on the little folk – on the forgotten, the down-trodden, the children with disabilities whom nobody pays attention to.

Many decades ago, a bright-eyed girl from the United States of America and a serious young man from India met, fell in love and settled in the foothills of the Himalayas. They had two home-made children and adopted their third. That third baby changed everything.

At the down-to-earth level, Moy Moy's presence in Jo and Ravi's life led to an organization that employs over a hundred individuals and has helped thousands of children. It led Jo to be the voice for many, many children with disabilities. It gives much needed solace and direction to hundreds of parents. It provides careers filled with purpose and meaning. Its efforts have had far-reaching legal ramifications.

At the non-rational, almost spiritual level, Moy Moy gave in unexpected and beautiful ways. To be non-speaking and yet share deep conversations, to be non-mobile and yet participate in long walks, dances and music, to be completely dependent on people like Manju, Sunita, Hema, Deepa, Naina and Shivani as caregivers for everything – from feeding through a tube, to changing your diapers – and yet have *them* feel grateful for the opportunity and the friendship: these are profound things. They are also not limited to her life-span. Saint John Chrysostom, during the Byzantine Empire, was the Archbishop of Constantinople. Across more than two thousand years his words ring true for Moy:

> 'Those whom we love and lose are no longer where they were. They are now wherever we are.'[351]

Moy Moy's life had effects far beyond her or anyone else's reckoning. It continues to do so – with joy, colour and much laughter.

14

A Way of Looking at the World

Photography involves taking a stance. The click of a shutter decides what the photographer seeks to capture. Even when the photograph is of real life on a busy street and not a carefully created composition in a studio, the photographer has determined what's included – and what's left out.

Jo thinks of herself as a writer and photographer. And there is much that she has chosen to leave out at Latika. What she chose to leave in, though, is worthy of note. Jo started Latika for her daughter, Moy Moy. It grew and embraced hundreds of children with disabilities in Dehradun. It influenced special educators, therapists, non-profits and families around the country. In its two and a half decades of existence, certain ways of doing took shape.

So, while this can be seen as the story of a particular mother and her child, or the story of a single non-profit organization, it transcends both descriptions. It holds lessons for us as individuals *and* for the organizations or companies we run. Here are some for you to consider.

Cultivate joy

Joy is almost mandated at Latika. The organization takes its work and responsibility to children with disabilities very seriously. But nobody said it cannot be done with laughter and good cheer, right? For example, Latika-children learn balance, numbers, how to share, coordination and much more through ... playing hopscotch.

You can't clench your teeth and achieve joy. It is a miraculous by-product. At Latika you see a quiet joy, a patient joy, a deeply fulfilling joy.

Non-profits that work with the disabled or the poor are often perceived as doing 'noble work.' As Jo writes, '"You are doing such noble work," people always say solemnly as they tour our school. "It must take so much patience to work with these children." We smile and nod and don't say anything. If people are determined to see us as saints, whatever we say will just be used as more evidence of what they already believe. But the truth is: we have never had so much fun in our lives.'[352]

Re-define wealth

At Latika, wealth springs from the very essence of life: The laughter of a child. The gleam in a teacher's eye when, after weeks of hard work, a child with cerebral palsy carefully reaches out and grasps an object. A child with autism chortling with laughter at the sheer joy of a balloon's flight.

Wealth comes from respect for each other, regardless of organizational hierarchy and economic class. At Latika, everyone is called 'Bhaiya' or 'Didi.' Ajay Sharma, long-time volunteer from the United Kingdom, remarks, 'The Bhaiya-Didi naming: even if you are pretending at the beginning, it eventually shifts your mindset. Behaviour and mindset are a two-way street. It is Latika's major strength. Long may it last.'[353]

Latika's wealth is manifested in how the employees banded together and worked relentlessly through the pandemic, devising way after ingenious way to reach parents in need. These are riches indeed.

Give wholeheartedly

Be generous, with ideas, skills and time. Latika poured a lot of its learning into creating an early intervention model that reaches children with disabilities when they are still babies. Catch them young, intervene with medical diagnosis and therapy. Support the parents, emotionally and with detailed lesson plans.

Instead of labelling it as proprietorial and hoarding the model, Latika shared it freely with others: no holding back, especially of things that are life-changing.

Keep the spirit alive, uplifted – full of dignity and fun. Mamta Govil has worked at Latika, is close friends with Jo, and is the current president of the board, so she brings a lot of insight when she says: 'The positive glow of energy, the deep concern and love for the children, the endeavour to do better for the children is really deep and doesn't seem to go away. Everyone who joins is caught up in the spirit. And considering it's now twenty-five years old, it's not jaded.'[354]

Love conquers all

What do you do when there are inevitable setbacks? Working with children with disabilities as Latika does means cultivating the patience to work at a different pace. It trains you to appreciate small changes: a boy being able to stand in line, even for ten seconds. It allows you to work over years on one particular achievement, like a girl who no longer spits at people, after three years. In turn, it builds a way to see and appreciate the small details that others might easily miss.

The love of the employees for the children is the beating heart of Latika. Wiping saliva dribbling down a child's face, holding a small hand to navigate a bump on the road, a home visit to follow up on menstrual lessons, the genuine smiles, high-fives and hugs that greet the children every morning: love shines through it all.

'Special needs are part of (our life's) journey. We don't get to choose when they will arrive or how they will manifest,' writes Jo in the Latika Calendar for 2008.

'All we are in charge of is how we handle them ... It's a journey of discovery, of joy and of sorrow and we set out on it alone, yet mysteriously together, united by the road and our shared humanity.

And when we meet with the inevitable diversions, missed turns and unexpected scenic routes, let's greet them for what they really are: tour guides from beyond, sent with directions, fuel and maps to that inclusive country for which we all yearn.'[355]

Acknowledgements

Writers are lucky; we get to know incredible people. In my case: Jo McGowan and Ravi Chopra. From 2019 to now, we have had meandering conversations, delicious meals, moving interviews and much laughter. Giants in their respective fields, they are inspiring people to know. Their home is aptly named Friendship House.

The parents at Latika gave me the precious gift of their time. I was touched by their openness, acceptance and quiet determination. A deep bow of appreciation and respect to Deepa Gehlot, Kusum Rawat, Mahindar Singh Kumar, Neelam Rawat, Savita Purohit, Sunita Chauhan.

Latika staff, working with children with disabilities, take on some of life's hardest challenges with joy and skill. I learnt much from Aarti Nair, Ashok Mamgain,

Harikala (Hema) Sharma, Kirti Chauhan, Manju Subedi, Manju Singhania, Megha Girdhar, Mohita Kapoor, Namita Jain, Prem Singh, Pooja Panwar, Rashi Bhatnagar, Rizwan Ali, Sandeep Khanna, Shaila Faliero, Shivani Kapoor, Shubha Nagesh, Sumita Nanda and Sunita Singh. Sumita helped get many things done, and Aravind Uniyal ensured the data stayed up-to-date.

In Latika's wider orbit I am grateful to Ajay Sharma, Anne Bruce, Dunu Roy, Ena Gaur, Paula Hughes, Preeti Kirbat, Ritu Arora Jain, Sanjay Sondhi, Sebastian Gruschke and Vibha Krishnamurthy. Some were brief, while others spoke over multiple interviews with far ranging discussions on books read and ideas explored. All of them gave me insights into Jo and how Latika functions.

Mamta Govil, warm and generous, is another friend made through this book. After careening all over Dehradun in her vintage Maruti, I'd come back and Jo would say, 'She took you where?!'

It cannot be easy being the children of Jo and Ravi. There is so much to live up to. Cathleen and Anand were able to sift through memories of their childhood with their sister while also being insightful about their parents. Other family members whose stories provided invaluable glimpses of Jo, Ravi and Moy Moy include Nutan Gupta, Margert

McNeill, Mary McGowan and Tom Synan.

Books find publishers in many ways. This one did through a nature walk and breakfast, an unexpected video chat and an introduction. Thank you so much, V. R. Ferose, Jaideep Rao and Akanksha Agarwal for paving the way with such generosity.

Robert Caro was lucky to have Robert Gottlieb. Tracy Kidder was lucky to have Richard Todd. That's how I feel about my editor Abhivyakti Singh. She's thoughtful, organized, and cares deeply about all aspects of an author's work. I don't know if she will put up with me for as long as Gottlieb and Todd were involved with their authors, but thus far it has been brilliant and I am optimistic.

Thomas Abraham, while still serving as managing director at Hachette India, made the time to write detailed responses to emails from someone he had never met. Such grace is inspiring.

Working with the rest of the team at Hachette India has been a treat. Thank you to Priyanka Sarkar and Rupal Vyas for copyediting and proofreading, Haider for typesetting, Anupama Manral and Sini Nair for getting things done behind the scenes, Priya Singh in Production and Abhishek Roy for handling marketing and outreach.

Covers play a profound role in linking writer to reader. Thank you, Harshvardhan Behura for ideas, execution and openness to collaboration.

Well-known people are hard pressed for time. Yet, many have made the time to write words of praise for this book. Thank you.

Some writers have studios to work in. I have my dining table, cafés and Evita, angel in disguise. She not only gave me a key to her villa but also stocked it with macadamia nuts, dark chocolate and high-quality coffee. Much of the rewriting of this book happened at her place.

A big thank-you to my parents, my other parents (in-law), the rest of the extended family and friends-who-are-family. You know who you are. Thank you for the chai sessions, meals, companionship and for tolerating the occasional rants!

My husband gave his first all-in-Hindi talk at one of Latika's Annual Day gatherings. Around that time, I had been mooching around, wondering what my next book should be. One day at breakfast, we both looked at each other suddenly, struck by the same idea: 'The next one should be Jo and Ravi's story and Jo's work at Latika!' Shreedhar has been there through it all, reading first drafts, editing last submissions, calmly navigating through my inevitable writerly crises. In the years it has taken this book to materialize, our daughter Kimaya has gone from a young child playing Lego as I interviewed Jo and Ravi to a teenager reading their copy of *Daddy Long Legs*. She has cheered me every step of the way.

This book starts with a dedication to Moy Moy. Much of what is contained in these pages is because of her. It is only fitting that I end by thanking her, for all that she brought into *my* life.

Appendix: Reaching Latika and Similar Organizations in India

Latika

https://latikaroy.org/donate/
113/1, Vasant Vihar, Dehradun 248001
Telephone: +91 135 276 1014 / +91 84390 00110

Online donations

https://latikaroy.org/donate/ https://give.do/nonprofits/latika-roy-memorial-foundation

Other organizations in India that work with children with disabilities

Bengaluru

Mitti Café (https://www.mitticafe.org/)

Delhi

Action for Autism (http://www.autism-india.org/)

Mumbai

Ummeed (https://ummeed.org/)

Guwahati

Shishu Sarothi
https://shishusarothi.org/index.php

Goa

Sethu (https://sethu.in/)

Hyderabad

Nayi Disha (https://nayi-disha.org/)

Endnotes

Chapter 1: Here's Someone I'd Like You to Meet

1. Jo Chopra, 'Moy Moy's story, it never gets old' (blogpost), Latika, 11 June 2011, https://latikaroy.org/jo/2011/06/11/Moy Moys-story-it-never-gets-old/.
2. Jo Chopra, 'Magic in the pediatric ward,' (blogpost), Latika, 27 June 2011, https://latikaroy.org/jo/2011/06/27/magic-in-the-pediatric-ward/.
3. Jo Chopra, 'Magic in the pediatric ward,' (blogpost), Latika, 27 June 2011, https://latikaroy.org/jo/2011/06/27/magic-in-the-pediatric-ward/.
4. Tom Kegelman, Moy Moy's third memorial meeting on Zoom, August 2021.
5. A 2019 UNESCO report states 7.8 million children with disabilities in India. However, those who work in disabilities feel the number is too low (given India's population). Instead, the number most used is 71 million in the World Health Organization's estimation

of 16 percent of the world's population having a disability and India's number of children under 18. Please note that this is an approximation and not an exact number. https://www.who.int/news-room/fact-sheets/detail/disability-and-health; https://www.statista.com/topics/9677/children-in-india.

Numbers cross-checked with Latika.

6. Neelam Rawat, interview by author, Dehradun, 29 November 2022.
7. Numbers calculated by author from Latika's annual reports. Estimates are based on conservative assumptions, to minimize double-counting among Latika's centres. Updated numbers from Arvind Uniyal, Data Analyst, Latika, 3 June 2023 and 29 April, 2025.
8. Ashok Mamgain, interview by author, Dehradun, 30 September 2019.
9. Jo Chopra, 'Moy Moy's story, it never gets old' (blogpost), 11 June 2011, https://latikaroy.org/jo/2011/06/11/Moy Moys-story-it-never-gets-old/.

Chapter 2: Garam Chai, Anyone?

10. Harikala (Hema) Sharma, interview by author, Dehradun, 27 May 2019.
11. Harikala (Hema) Sharma, interview by author, Dehradun, 27 May 2019.
12. Harikala (Hema) Sharma, interview by author, Dehradun, 27 May 2019.
13. Harikala (Hema) Sharma, interview by author, Dehradun, 27 May 2019.

14. Harikala (Hema) Sharma, interview by author, Dehradun, 27 May 2019.
15. Harikala (Hema) Sharma, interview by author, Dehradun, 27 May 2019.
16. Harikala (Hema) Sharma, interview by author, Dehradun, 27 May 2019.
17. Dr Tom Synan, telephone interview by author, New Hampshire, United States, 22 November 2020.
18. Jo Chopra, interviews by author, Dehradun, May 2019-December 2022.
19. Informal conversation, Chopra-McGowan household, Dehradun, 2019.
20. Dr Mary McGowan, telephone interview by author, New Hampshire, United States, 8 November 2020.
21. Jo Chopra, interviews by author, Dehradun, May 2019-December 2022.
22. Anand-Chopra-McGowan, telephone interview by author, London, 1 October 2020.
23. Dr Tom Synan, telephone interview by author, New Hampshire, United States, 22 November 2020.
24. Anand-Chopra-McGowan, telephone interview by author, London, 1 October 2020.
25. Anand-Chopra-McGowan, telephone interview by author, London, 1 October 2020.
26. Mamta Govil, interview by author, Dehradun, 15 July 2019.
27. Dr Cathleen Chopra-McGowan, telephone interview by author, Chicago, April 2020.
28. Dr Cathleen Chopra-McGowan, telephone interview by author, Chicago, April 2020.

29. Dr Cathleen Chopra-McGowan, telephone interview by author, Chicago, April 2020.
30. Anand Chopra-McGowan, telephone interview by author, London, 1 October 2020.
31. Nutan Gupta, telephone interview by author, Connecticut, United States, 17 October, 2020.
32. Anand Chopra-McGowan, telephone interview by author, London, 1 October 2020.
33. Latika Roy Foundation Annual Report, Latika, 2020-2021, page 3. Updated number from Aravind Uniyal at Latika, 30 April, 2025
34. Harikala (Hema) Sharma, interview by author, Dehradun, 27 May 2019.
35. Ravi Chopra, interviews by author, Dehradun, June, October, 2019.
36. Shivani Kapoor, interview by author, Dehradun, 17 July 2019.
37. Cathleen Chopra-McGowan, 'Magic in the Pediatric Ward,' (blogpost), Latika, 27 June 2011, https://latikaroy.org/jo/2011/06/27/magic-in-the-pediatric-ward/.
38. Cathleen Chopra-McGowan, 'Magic in the Pediatric Ward,' (blogpost), Latika, 27 June 2011, https://latikaroy.org/jo/2011/06/27/magic-in-the-pediatric-ward/.
39. Jo Chopra, interviews by author, Dehradun, May 2019-December 2022.
40. Jo Chopra, interviews by author, Dehradun, May 2019-December 2022.
41. Shivani Kapoor, interview by author, Dehradun, 17 July 2019.
42. Manju Subedi, interview by author, Dehradun, 30 November, 2022.

43. Shivani Kapoor, interview by author, Dehradun, 17 July 2019.
44. Jo Chopra, 'This is how we learn,' (blogpost), Latika, 23 July 2015, https://latikaroy.org/jo/2015/07/23/and-this-is-how-we-learn/.
45. Rizwan Ali, interview by author, Dehradun, 27 September 2019.
46. Rizwan Ali, interview by author, Dehradun, 27 September 2019.
47. Rizwan Ali, interview by author, Dehradun, 27 September 2019.
48. Harikala (Hema) Sharma, interview by author, Dehradun, 27 May 2019.
49. Cathleen Chopra-McGowan, 'Magic in the Pediatric ward,' (blogpost), Latika, 27 June 2011.
50. Harikala (Hema) Sharma, interview by author, Dehradun, 27 May 2019.
51. Jo Chopra, 'Expertise,' (blogpost), Latika, 2 April 2010, https://latikaroy.org/jo/2010/04/02/expertise/.
52. Jo Chopra, 'Feeding tube rules,' (blogpost), Latika, 27 June 2011, https://latikaroy.org/jo/2011/06/27/feeding-tubes-rule/.
53. Jo Chopra, 'Rules for life with Moy Moy,' (blogpost), Latika, 4 February 2015, https://latikaroy.org/jo/2015/02/04/rules-for-life-with-Moy Moy/.
54. Shaila Faleiro, telephone interview by author, Bangalore, 23 November 2021.
55. Shaila Faleiro, telephone interview by author, Bangalore, 23 November 2021.
56. Shaila Faleiro, telephone interview by author, Bangalore, 23 November 2021.

57. Shaila Faleiro, telephone interview by author, Bangalore, 23 November 2021.

Chapter 3: Designing for the Most Vulnerable

58. Jo Chopra, talk at IIM-Kashipur, 22 May 2019, https://www.youtube.com/watch?v=xKiC4IoNk3k.
59. World Health Organization, 'Disability Fact sheet,' March 2023, https://www.who.int/news-room/fact-sheets/detail/disability-and-health. Numbers cross-checked with Latika.
60. Abhishek Anicca, Shubha Nagesh, 'How 2021 can be more disability-inclusive,' Devex.com, 8 January 2021, https://www.devex.com/news/opinion-how-2021-can-be-more-disability-inclusive-98869.
61. Ena Gaur, telephone interview by author, Noida, 22 February 2021.
62. Ena Gaur, telephone interview by author, Noida, 22 February 2021.
63. Harper B.D., et al.,'Where are the paediatricians? An international survey to understand the global paediatric workforce,' *BMJ Paediatric Open*, 31 January 2019, https://www.ncbi.nlm.nih.gov/pmc/articles/PMC6361365/.
64. Sandeep Khanna, interview by author, Dehradun, 17 July 2019.
65. Sandeep Khanna, interview by author, Dehradun, 17 July 2019.
66. Gubbara, Latika Annual reports, Latika Roy Foundation web-site, https://latikaroy.org/gubbara/. Updated from Arvind Uniya, 30 April 2025.

67. Jo Chopra, interview by author, Dehradun, May 2023.
68. Paula Hughes, telephone and email interviews by author, England, 25 September, 11 October 2020.
69. Pooja Panwar, interview by author, Dehradun 30 November, 2022.
70. Pooja Panwar, interview by author, Dehradun 30 November, 2022.
71. Latika Roy Foundation Annual Report, Latika, 2020-2021, page 3. Updated by Arvind Uniyal, Latika, 30 April 2025.
72. United Nations Enable, 'Fact sheet on Persons with Disability,' https://www.un.org/disabilities/documents/toolaction/pwdfs.pdf. Numbers cross-checked with Latika.
73. Neelam Rawat, interview by author, Dehradun, 29 November 2022.
74. Anne Bruce, telephone and video interviews by author, Scotland, 8 November 2020, 14 June, 2021.
75. Latika Roy Foundation Annual Report, Latika, 2020-2021, 3. Updated by Arvind Uniyal, Latika Data Analyst, May 2023 and 30 April, 2025.
76. Paula Hughes, telephone and email interviews by author, 25 September, 11 October 2020
77. Paula Hughes, telephone and email interviews by author, 25 September, 11 October 2020
78. Ena Gaur, telephone interview by author, Noida, 22 February 2021.
79. Neelam Rawat, interview by author, Dehradun, 29 November 2022.
80. Manju Subedi, interview by author, Dehradun, 30 November 2022.

81. Manju Subedi, interview by author, Dehradun, 30 November 2022.
82. Manju Subedi, interview by author, Dehradun, 30 November 2022.
83. Manju Subedi, interview by author, Dehradun, 30 November 2022.
84. Manju Subedi, interview by author, Dehradun, 30 November 2022.
85. Sunita Singh, interview by author, Dehradun, 30 November 2022.
86. Sunita Singh, interview by author, Dehradun, 30 November 2022.
87. Sunita Singh, interview by author, Dehradun, 30 November 2022.
88. Latika Roy Foundation Annual Report, Latika, 2020-2021.
89. Sunita Singh, interview by author, Dehradun, 30 November 2022.
90. Prem Singh, interview by author, Dehradun, 30 November 2022.
91. Latika Roy Foundation Annual Report, Latika, 2020-2021, 3. Updated by Arvind Uniyal, Data Analyst, Latika, May 2023.
92. Prem Singh, interview by author, Dehradun, 30 November 2022.
93. Prem Singh, interview by author, Dehradun, 30 November 2022.
94. United Nations Enable, 'Fact sheet on Persons with Disability,' https://www.un.org/disabilities/documents/toolaction/pwdfs.pdf.

95. Prem Singh, interview by author, Dehradun, 30 November 2022.
96. Mahindar Singh Kumar, interview by author, Dehradun, 30 November 2022.
97. Mahindar Singh Kumar, interview by author, Dehradun, 30 November 2022.
98. Mahindar Singh Kumar, interview by author, Dehradun, 30 November 2022.
99. Celia Kwan, Mojgan Gitimoghaddam and Jean-Paul Collet, 'Effects of Social Isolation and Loneliness in Children with Neurodevelopmental Disabilities: A Scoping Review,' *Brain Sciences*, vol. 10, no. 11 (November 2020), 786.
100. Prem Singh, interview by author, Dehradun, 30 November 2022.
101. Latika Roy Foundation Annual Report, Latika, 2020-2021, page 3. Updated by Arvind Uniyal, Latika, 30 April, 2025.
102. Kusum Rawat, interview by author, Dehradun, 30 November 2022.
103. Kusum Rawat, interview by author, Dehradun, 30 November 2022.
104. Ena Gaur, telephone interview by author, Noida, 22 February 2021.

Chapter 4: Seeds That Blossom Later

105. Isabella Tree, *Wilding: The return of nature to a British farm* (London: Picador, 2018), 121-122.
106. Jo Chopra, interviews by author, Dehradun, May 2019-December 2022.

107. Nicola, is sadly, quite ill, and so unable to interview for this book.
108. Sumita Nanda, interview by author, Dehradun, 17 July 2019.
109. Sumita Nanda, interview by author, Dehradun, 17 July 2019.
110. Sumita Nanda, interview by author, Dehradun, 17 July 2019.
111. Mireille De La Sablonnière-Griffin, et al., 'Child maltreatment investigations and substantiations in child protection services: Factors distinguishing children with intellectual disabilities,' Disability Health, October 2021, https://pubmed.ncbi.nlm.nih.gov/34144896/.
112. Sumita Nanda, interview by author, Dehradun, 17 July 2019.
113. Dr Ajay Sharma, 'Latika Roy Foundation Evaluation Report,' April, 2019.
114. Jo Chopra, 'Protecting children is hard work,' (blogpost), Latika, 29 July 2017, https://latikaroy.org/jo/2017/07/29/protecting-children-hard-work/.
115. Sumita Nanda, interview by author, Dehradun, 17 July 2019.
116. 'IFC PPPs in Health,' International Finance Corporation, https://www.ifc.org/wps/wcm/connect/Industry_EXT_Content/IFC_External_Corporate_Sit e/PPP/Priorities/Health/.
117. Nasrin Joudyian, et al., 'Public-private partnerships in primary health care: a scoping review,' BMC Health Services Research, January 2021, https://

bmchealthservres.biomedcentral.com/articles/10.1186/s12913-020-05979-9.
118. Dr Sebastian Gruschke, telephone interview by author, Amsterdam, 12 December 2021.
119. Dr Sebastian Gruschke, telephone interview by author, Amsterdam, 12 December 2021.
120. Dr Sebastian Gruschke, telephone interview by author, Amsterdam, 12 December 2021.
121. Jo Chopra, 'Edmund Cluett guruji,' (blogpost), Latika, 13 May 2008, https://latikaroy.org/jo/2008/05/13/edmund-cluett-guruji/.
122. Paula Hughes, telephone and email interview by author, 25 September and 11 October, 2020.
123. Paula Hughes, telephone and email interview by author, 25 September and 11 October, 2020.
124. Jo Chopra, 'An Easter resurrection,' (blogpost), Latika, 22 April 2017, https://latikaroy.org/jo/2017/04/22/an-easter-resurrection/.
125. Ravi Chopra, interviews by author, Dehradun, June, October, 2019.
126. Jo and Paula, both avid readers, were at that time, deep into historical novels by Patrick O'Brian; novels based on the British Navy in the eighteenth century. So, their chatter was full of nautical references: 'Avast, ye swabs!' and things happening at 'a rate of knots.' Jo Chopra, 'Worse things happen at sea,' Jo's blog, Latika, 16 June 2014, https://latikaroy.org/jo/2014/06/16/worse-things-happen-at-sea/.
127. Paula Hughes, 'Change is often slow' (blogpost), Latika, 27 June 2011, https://latikaroy.org/jo/2011/06/27/change-is-often-slow/.

128. Paula Hughes, 'Change is often slow' (blogpost), Latika, 27 June 2011, https://latikaroy.org/jo/2011/06/27/change-is-often-slow/.
129. Paula Hughes, telephone and email interviews by author, 25 September, 11 October 2020.
130. Petra Warreyn, Sara van der Paelt, Herbert Roeyers, 'Social-communicative abilities as treatment goals for preschool children with autism spectrum disorder: the importance of imitation, joint attention, and play,' *Developmental Medicine and Child Neurology*, April 2014, Volume 56, Issue 8, https://doi.org/10.1111/dmcn.12455.
131. Jo Chopra, 'An Easter resurrection' (blogpost), Latika, 22 April 2017, https://latikaroy.org/jo/2017/04/22/an-easter-resurrection/.
132. Paula Hughes, telephone and email interviews by author, 25 September and 11 October 2020.
133. Paula Hughes, telephone and email interviews by author, 25 September and 11 October 2020.
134. Charles Duhigg, *The Power of Habit* (London: William Heinemann, 2012), 156.
135. Charles Duhigg, *The Power of Habit* (London: William Heinemann, 2012), 156.
136. Masaaki Mai, *Kaizen: The Key to Japan's Competitive Success* (New York: Random House, 1986), 173.
137. John Shook, 'How to Change a Culture: Lessons from NUMMI,' *MIT Sloan Management Review*, Winter 2010.
138. Ravi Chopra, interview by author, Dehradun, May 2023.
139. Sandeep Khanna, interview by author, Dehradun, 17 July 2019.

140. Jo Chopra, 'An Easter resurrection' (blogpost), Latika, 22 April 2017, https://latikaroy.org/jo/2017/04/22/an-easter-resurrection/.

Chapter 5: What's with the Name?

141. Dunu Roy, telephone interview by author, Delhi, 23 November 2021.
142. Ravi Chopra, interviews by author, Dehradun, June, October 2019.
143. Dunu Roy, telephone interview by author, Delhi, 23 November 2021.

Chapter 6: A Girl from Fall River, A Boy from Charni Road

144. Jo Chopra, interviews by author, Dehradun, May 2019-December 2022.
145. James M. Lindsay, 'Twenty best Vietnam protest songs,' Council on Foreign Relations, 5 March 2015, https://www.cfr.org/blog/twenty-best-vietnam-protest-songs.
146. Continental Walk for Disarmament and Social Justice Records, 1975-1978, Swarthmore College Peace Collection, DG 135. http://www.swarthmore.edu/Library/peace//DG100-150/dg135cwdsj.htm.
147. Swarthmore College Peace Collection, Swarthmore College, https://www.swarthmore.edu/library/peace/DG100-150/dg135cwdsj.htm.
148. Bob Sabath, 'The Continental Walk,' *Sojourners Magazine*, Feb 1976, https://sojo.net/magazine/february-1976/continental-walk.

149. Jo Chopra, interviews by author, Dehradun, May 2019-December 2022.
150. Jo Chopra, interviews by author, Dehradun, May 2019-December 2022.
151. Jo Chopra, interviews by author, Dehradun, May 2019-December 2022.
152. Jo Chopra, interviews by author, Dehradun, May 2019-December 2022.
153. Jo Chopra, interviews by author, Dehradun, May 2019-December 2022.
154. Ravi Chopra, interviews by author, Dehradun, June, October 2019.
155. Ravi Chopra, interviews by author, Dehradun, June, October 2019.
156. Jo Chopra, interviews by author, Dehradun, May 2019-December 2022.
157. Ravi Chopra, interviews by author, Dehradun, June, October, 2019.
158. Ravi Chopra, interviews by author, Dehradun, June, October, 2019.
159. Ravi Chopra, interviews by author, Dehradun, June, October, 2019.
160. Ravi Chopra, interviews by author, Dehradun, June, October, 2019.
161. Nutan Gupta, telephone interview by author, Connecticut, United States, 17 October, 2020.
162. Paul Grimes, 'Protests Rise on Curbs in India,' *New York Times*, 8 March 1976, https://www.nytimes.com/1976/03/08/archives/new-jersey-pages-protests-

rising-on-curbs-in-india-gandhi-regimes.html.

163. Paul Grimes, 'Protests Rise on Curbs in India,' *New York Times*, 8 March 1976, https://www.nytimes.com/1976/03/08/archives/new-jersey-pages-protests-rising-on-curbs-in-india-gandhi-regimes.html.
164. Ravi Chopra, interviews by author, Dehradun, June, October 2019.
165. Jo Chopra, interviews by author, Dehradun, May 2019-December 2022.
166. Ravi Chopra, interviews by author, Dehradun, June, October 2019.
167. Jo Chopra, interviews by author, Dehradun, May 2019-December
168. Jo Chopra, interviews by author, Dehradun, May 2019-December
169. Dr Mary McGowan, telephone interview by author, New Hampshire, United States, 8 November 2020.
170. Nutan Gupta, telephone interview by author, Connecticut, United States, 17 October 2020.
171. Jo Chopra, interviews by author, Dehradun, May 2019-December 2022.
172. Nutan Gupta, telephone interview by author, Connecticut, United States, 17 October 2020
173. Jo Chopra, interviews by author, Dehradun, May 2019-December 2022.
174. Ena Gaur, telephone interview by author, Noida, 22 February 2021.
175. Dr Cathleen Chopra-McGowan, telephone interview by author, Chicago, 6 April 2020.

Chapter 7: What is Worth Working On

176. Anne Bruce, telephone interviews by author, Scotland, 8 November 2020, 14 June 2021.
177. Anne Bruce, telephone interviews by author, Scotland, 8 November 2020, 14 June 2021.
178. Anne Bruce, telephone interviews by author, Scotland, 8 November 2020, 14 June 2021.
179. Anne Bruce, telephone interviews by author, Scotland, 8 November 2020, 14 June 2021.
180. Anne Bruce, telephone interviews by author, Scotland, 8 November 2020, 14 June 2021.
181. Sunita Singh, interview by author, Dehradun, 30 November 2022.
182. Sunita Singh, interview by author, Dehradun, 30 November 2022.
183. Anne Bruce, telephone interviews by author, Scotland, 8 November 2020, 14 June 2021.
184. 'Physicians per 1000 people: India,' World Health Organization's Global Health Workforce Statistics, The World Bank, 2019. https://data.worldbank.org/indicator/SH.MED.PHYS.ZS?contextual=max&end=2019&location s=IN&start=1960&view=chart.
185. Dr Ajay Sharma, interview by author, Dehradun, 15 September 2019.
186. Dr Ajay Sharma, interview by author, Dehradun, 15 September 2019.
187. Dr Ajay Sharma, interview by author, Dehradun, 15 September 2019.
188. Savitha Purohit, interview by author, Dehradun, 29 November 2022.

189. Savitha Purohit, interview by author, Dehradun, 29 November 2022.
190. Savitha Purohit, interview by author, Dehradun, 29 November 2022.
191. Savitha Purohit, interview by author, Dehradun, 29 November 2022.
192. Savitha Purohit, interview by author, Dehradun, 29 November 2022.
193. Savitha Purohit, interview by author, Dehradun, 29 November 2022.
194. Dr Ajay Sharma, 'Latika Roy Foundation Evaluation Report,' April 2019, page 2.
195. Dr Ajay Sharma, interview by author, Dehradun, September 2019.
196. Dr Ajay Sharma, interview by author, Dehradun, September, 2019.
197. Dr Ajay Sharma, interview by author, Dehradun, September, 2019.
198. Carsten Tams, 'The Co-Creation Imperative: How to Make Organizational Change Collaborative,' *Forbes*, 11 February, 2018, https://www.forbes.com/sites/carstentams/2018/02/11/the-co-creation-imperative-how-to-make-organizational-change-collaborative/.
199. Dr Ajay Sharma, interview by author, Dehradun, September, 2019.

Chapter 8: The Obsession with Scale

200. Dr Ajay Sharma, interview by author, Dehradun, September, 2019.
201. Names have been changed for privacy.

202. Jo Chopra, 'The law works if we make it work' (blogpost), Latika, 20 June 2016, https://latikaroy.org/jo/2016/06/20/the-law-works-if-we-make-it-work/.
203. Jo Chopra, 'The law works if we make it work' (blogpost), Latika, 20 June 2016, https://latikaroy.org/jo/2016/06/20/the-law-works-if-we-make-it-work/.
204. Rizwan Ali, interview by author, Dehradun, 27 September 2019.
205. Jo Chopra, 'The law works if we make it work' (blogpost), Latika, 20 June 2016, https://latikaroy.org/jo/2016/06/20/the-law-works-if-we-make-it-work/.
206. Rizwan Ali, interview by author, Dehradun, 27 September 2019.
207. Sakshi vs Union of India, 2004.
208. Rizwan Ali, interview by author, Dehradun, 27 September 2019.
209. Rizwan Ali, interview by author, Dehradun, 27 September 2019.
210. The amount has gone up to seven lakhs with the Nirbhaya case. The Nirbhaya case was a gang rape and fatal assault that took place in Delhi in December 2012. The victim was a twenty-two-year-old physiotherapy intern, who was travelling with a male friend in a bus. She was beaten, gang-raped, and tortured by six men in the bus, including the driver. Her friend was severely beaten. She died in hospital, succumbing to her injuries. The case generated national and international coverage and led to public protests in the country. Indian law prohibits the press from publishing a rape victim's name so the case became

known as Nirbhaya, which means fearless, a symbol of women's resistance to violence. https://en.wikipedia.org/wiki/2012_Delhi_gang_rape_and_murder, https://timesofindia.indiatimes.com/india/what-is-nirbhaya-case/articleshow/72868430.cms.

211. Ena Gaur, telephone interview by author, Noida, 22 February 2021.
212. Shivani Kapoor, interview by author, Dehradun, 17 July 2019.
213. Shivani Kapoor, interview by author, Dehradun, 17 July 2019.
214. Shivani Kapoor, interview by author, Dehradun, 17 July 2019.
215. Tripti Lahiri, *Maid in India* (Delhi: Aleph Book Company, 2017), xii.
216. Nonprofit HR, '2022 Social Impact Talent Retention Practices Survey', 2022, nonprofit.com/2022talentretentionsurvey.
217. Anne Bruce, telephone interviews by author, Scotland, 8 November 2020, 14 June 2021.
218. Jo Chopra, interviews by author, Dehradun, May 2019-December 2022.
219. Shivani Kapoor, interview by author, Dehradun, 17 July 2019.
220. Jo Chopra, interviews by author, Dehradun, May 2019-December 2022.

Chapter 9: The Obsession with Scale

221. Jo Chopra, interviews by author, May 2019-December 2022

222. Ravi Chopra, interview by author, Dehradun, May 2023.
223. Author's emphasis.
224. Latika Roy Foundation Background Note, 'Who We Are and What We Do,' Latika, 2019.
225. 'Count Me In,' Dasra, March 2019, page 66.
226. 'Count Me In,' Dasra, March 2019, page 55.
227. Sunita Chauhan, interview by author, Dehradun, 29 November 2022.
228. Sunita Chauhan, interview by author, Dehradun, 29 November 2022.
229. Sunita Chauhan, interview by author, Dehradun, 29 November 2022.
230. Sunita Chauhan, interview by author, Dehradun, 29 November 2022.
231. Sunita Chauhan, interview by author, Dehradun, 29 November 2022.
232. Sunita Chauhan, interview by author, Dehradun, 29 November 2022.
233. Sunita Chauhan, interview by author, Dehradun, 29 November 2022.
234. Shubha Nagesh, telephone interview by author, 17 November 2021.
235. Dr Sebastian Gruschke, telephone interview by author, Amsterdam, 12 December 2021.
236. Dr Shubha Nagesh, telephone interview by author, Dehradun, 17 November 2021.
237. Aarti Nair, exchange on WhatsApp with author, 14 January 2023.
238. Latika Roy Foundation Annual Report, Latika, 2020-2021, page 4.

239. Jo Chopra, interviews by author, Dehradun, May 2019-December 2022.

240. 'State of the Education Report for India: Children with Disabilities,' UNESCO, 2019, page102.

Chapter 10: A Matter of Faith

241. Cathleen Chopra-McGowan, 'Magic in the Pediatric Ward,' (blogpost), Latika Roy Foundation, 27 June 2011, https://latikaroy.org/jo/2011/06/27/magic-in-the-pediatric-ward/.

242. Zeeshan Shaikh, 'What a study in 2013 revealed about interfaith marriages in India,' *The Indian Express*, 22 October 2020, https://indianexpress.com/article/explained/explained-what-a-2013-study-revealed-about-interfaith-marriages-6742991/.

243. Jo Chopra, interviews by author, Dehradun, May 2019-December 2022.

244. Anand Chopra-McGowan, telephone interview by author, London, 1 October 2020.

245. Dr Cathleen Chopra-McGowan, telephone interview by author, Chicago, 6 April 2020.

246. Anand Chopra-McGowan, telephone interview by author, London, 1 October 2020.

247. Jo Chopra, interviews by author, Dehradun, May 2019-December 2022.

248. Stapleton, G., 'Qualifying choice: ethical reflection on the scope of prenatal screening,' *Medical Health Care and Philosophy*, 2017, https://doi.org/10.1007/s11019-016-9725-2.

249. Stapleton, G., 'Qualifying choice: ethical reflection on the scope of prenatal screening,' *Medical Health Care and Philosophy*, 2017, https://doi.org/10.1007/s11019-016-9725-2.
250. Jo Chopra, interviews by author, Dehradun, May 2019-December 2022.
251. Jo Chopra, interviews by author, Dehradun, May 2019-December 2022.
252. Jo McGowan, 'Why I Stayed and Why I am Leaving,' *Commonweal*, 8 May 2019.
253. Jo Chopra, interviews by author, Dehradun, May 2019-December 2022.
254. Jo Chopra, interviews by author, Dehradun, May 2019-December 2022.
255. Jo Chopra, interviews by author, Dehradun, May 2019-December 2022.
256. Mother Teresa, *'The Joy in Loving: A Guide to Daily Life'* (New York: Penguin Compass, 1996).
257. Jo Chopra, interviews by author, Dehradun, May 2019-December 2022.
258. Jo Chopra, interviews by author, Dehradun, May 2019-December 2022.
259. Jo Chopra, TEDx Talk, https://www.ted.com/talks/jo_mcgowan_chopra_just_leap_the_net_will_appear.
260. Jo Chopra, interviews by author, Dehradun, May 2019-December 2022.
261. Jo Chopra, interviews by author, Dehradun, May 2019-December 2022.
262. Jo Chopra, interviews by author, Dehradun, May 2019-December 2022.

263. Jo Chopra, interviews by author, Dehradun, May 2019-December 2022.
264. 'Sermon on the Mount,' The Bible, Lesson 6, Matthew 6:25-34.
265. Walt Whitman, 'Miracles', https://poets.org/poem/miracles.
266. Phone call to author, 10 April 2022.

Chapter 11: Latika Grows Up

267. Dr Cathleen Chopra-McGowan, telephone interview by author, Chicago, 6 April 2020.
268. Anand Chopra-McGowan, telephone interview by author, London, 1 October 2020
269. Anand Chopra-McGowan, telephone interview by author, London, 1 October 2020
270. Nutan Gupta, telephone interview by author, Connecticut, United States, 17 October 2020.
271. In 2008, the first year Annual Reports were published for Latika, the expenditure was Rs 104,15,000. So, assuming a budget of about Rs 80,00,000 in 2005, Nutan's gift was substantial at an exchange rate of Rs 44 to the US dollar.
272. Jo Chopra, interview by author, May 2023.
273. Jo Chopra, interview by author, May 2023.
274. Jo Chopra, 'Act now why wait' (blogpost), Latika, 1 April 2016, https://latikaroy.org/jo/2016/04/01/1-in-68-act-now-why-wait/.
275. Dr Ajay Sharma, interview by author, Dehradun, September 2019.

276. Dr Ajay Sharma, interview by author, Dehradun, September 2019.

277. Jo Chopra, interviews by author, Dehradun, May 2019-December 2022.

278. Neelkamal Soares, et al., 'Developmental-behavioral pediatrics education in the United States: challenges in the midst of healthcare evolution,' *International Journal of Medical Education*, 2017, https://www.ncbi.nlm.nih.gov/pmc/articles/PMC5694693/.

279. Jo Chopra, interviews by author, Dehradun, May 2019-December 2022.

280. Dr Ajay Sharma, interview by author, Dehradun, September 2019.

281. Dr Ajay Sharma, interview by author, Dehradun, September 2019.

282. Jo Chopra, interview by author, May 2023.

283. Jo Chopra, interviews by author, May 2019-December 2022.

284. Dr Ajay Sharma, 'Latika Roy Foundation Evaluation Report,' April 2019, page 2.

285. Dr Shubha Nagesh, telephone interview by author, Dehradun, 17 November, 2021.

286. 'A New Era for Girls', UNICEF, 2020, 5, https://www.unicef.org/reports/new-era-for-girls-2020.

287. Dr Shubha Nagesh et al., 'Young Girls with Developmental Disabilities in the Himalayas,' *Journal for Disability Studies*, Vol 7, No. 2, 2021.

288. Shubha Nagesh, telephone interview by author, 17 November 2021.

289. Dr Ajay Sharma, 'Latika Roy Foundation Evaluation Report,' April 2019.

290. Ravi Chopra, interviews by author, Dehradun, June, October, 2019.
291. Dunu Roy, telephone interview by author, Delhi, 23 November 2021.
292. Dr Ajay Sharma, interview by author, Dehradun, September, 2019.
293. Ravi Chopra, interview by author, Dehradun, May, 2023.
294. Dana O'Donovan, Jarasa Kanok, 'It's time for real talk about leadership transitions,' *What's Next: Monitor Institute Blog*, 6 April 2022, https://www2.deloitte.com/us/en/blog/monitor-institute-blog/2022/nonprofit-leadership-transitions.html.
295. Ritu Arora Jain, telephone interview by author, Singapore, 21 March 2022.
296. Ravi Chopra, interviews by author, Dehradun, June, October, 2019.
297. Ravi Chopra, interviews by author, Dehradun, June, October, 2019.
298. Ritu Arora Jain, telephone interview by author, Singapore, 21 March 2022.
299. Ritu Arora Jain, telephone interview by author, Singapore, 21 March 2022.
300. Ravi Chopra, Jo Chopra, interviews by author, Dehradun, May 2019-May 2023.

Chapter 12: The Effect of a Virus

301. The number of deaths in India from Covid, while controversial, has been ascertained both by the World Health Organization, and by the globally relied on

Johns Hopkins University data: https://github.com/CSSEGISandData/COVID-19.

302. 'Covid: Disabled people account for six in 10 deaths in England last year,' BBC News, 11 February, 2021, https://www.bbc.com/news/uk-56033813.
303. Shubha Nagesh, 'Disabling Corona!' *International Health Policies*, 19 March 2020, https://www.internationalhealthpolicies.org/blogs/disabling-corona/.
304. Manju Subedi, interview by author, Dehradun, 30 November 2022.
305. Jo Chopra, 'Working throughout,' (blogpost), Latika, 1 May 2020, https://ltikaroy.org/jo/2020/05/01/shut-may-15-working-throughout/.
306. Manju Subedi, interview by author, Dehradun, 30 November 2022.
307. Manju Subedi, interview by author, Dehradun, 30 November 2022.
308. 'India rolls out the world's largest COVID-19 vaccination drive,' World Health Organization, January 2021.
309. https://vaccinate-india.in/dashboard.
310. Sarah Rotenberg, Shubha Nagesh, 'Many people with disabilities lack access to COVID-19 vaccines,' Devex.com, 8 June 2021, https://www.devex.com/news/opinion-many-people-with-disabilities-lack-access-to-covid-19-vaccines-100081.
311. Shubha Nagesh, telephone interview by author, 17 November 2021.
312. Neelam Rawat, interview by author, Dehradun, 29 November 2022.

313. Shubha Nagesh, telephone interview by author, 17 November 2021.
314. Sumita Nanda, interview by author, Dehradun, 30 November 2022.

Chapter 13: Where do we go from here?

315. W. S. Merwin, 'Separation' from *The Second Four Books of Poems* (Michigan: Copper Canyon Press, 1993).
316. Jo Chopra, interviews by author, Dehradun, May 2019-December 2022.
317. Deuteronomy 33:27, The Bible.
318. Jo Chopra, Moy Moy's Memorial, New Hampshire, 2019.
319. Shivani Kapoor, interview by author, Dehradun, 17 July 2019.
320. Shivani Kapoor, interview by author, Dehradun, 17 July 2019.
321. Shivani Kapoor, interview by author, Dehradun, 17 July 2019.
322. Shivani Kapoor, interview by author, Dehradun, 17 July 2019.
323. Shivani Kapoor, interview by author, Dehradun, 17 July 2019.
324. Ravi Chopra, Moy Moy's memorial service, New Hampshire, 2019.
325. Jo Chopra, 'The age of Moy Moy' (blogpost), Latika, 30 September 2019, https://latikaroy.org/jo/2019/09/30/age-Moy Moy/.
326. Jo Chopra, Moy Moy's Memorial, New Hampshire, 2019.

327. Jo Chopra, interviews by author, Dehradun, May 2019-December 2022.
328. Jo Chopra, interviews by author, Dehradun, May 2019-December 2022.
329. Mamta Govil, telephone interview by author, Dehradun, 23 March 2022.
330. Ravi Chopra, Moy Moy's memorial service, New Hampshire, 2019.
331. Jo Chopra, Moy Moy memorial service, New Hampshire, 2019.
332. Dr Ajay Sharma, interview by author, Dehradun, September 2019.
333. Dr Vibha Krishnamurthy, telephone interview by author, Mumbai, 8 May 2020.
334. Mamta Govil, telephone interview by author, Dehradun, 23 March 2022.
335. Dorothy Day, *The Long Loneliness: The Autobiography of the Legendary Catholic Social Activist* (San Francisco: Harper Collins, 1952), 286.
336. Anand Chopra-McGowan, telephone interview by author, London, 1 October, 2020.
337. The story is brought to life by Tom McCarthy in his 2015 feature film, *Spotlight*.
338. Jo Chopra, interviews by author, Dehradun, May 2019-December 2022.
339. Jo Chopra, interviews by author, Dehradun, May 2019-December 2022.
340. Jo Chopra, interviews by author, Dehradun, May 2019-December 2022.
341. Dr Aarti Nair, telephone interview by author, Connecticut, United States, 24 November 2022.

342. Mamta Govil, interview by author, Dehradun, 15 July 2019.
343. Dr Sebastian Gruschke, telephone interview by author, Amsterdam, 12 December 2021.
344. Dr Sebastian Gruschke, telephone interview by author, Amsterdam, 12 December 2021.
345. Jo Chopra, interview by author, Dehradun, May 2023.
346. Megha Girdhar, interview by author, Dehradun, September 2019.
347. Dunu Roy, telephone interview by author, Delhi, 23 November 2021.
348. Manju Subedi, interview by author, Dehradun, 1 December 2022.
349. Harikala (Hema) Sharma, interview by author, Dehradun, 27 May 2019.
350. Johns Hopkins data: https://gisanddata.maps.arcgis.com/apps/opsdashboard/index.html#/bda7594740fd402994234 67b48e9ecf6.
351. Jo Chopra, 'Orphaned at an advanced age' (blog post), https://latikaroy.org/jo/2016/06/21/orphaned-at-an-advanced-age/.

Chapter 14: A Way of Looking at the World

352. Jo Chopra, essay in the Latika Calendar, 2000.
353. Dr Ajay Sharma, interview by author, Dehradun, September 2019.
354. Mamta Govil, interview by author, Dehradun, 15 July 2019.
355. Jo Chopra, Latika Calendar, 2008.

WITH A FOREWORD BY
HIS HOLINESS THE DALAI LAMA

The Invisible Majority

INDIA'S ABLED DISABLED

C.K. MEENA
V.R. FEROSE

MORE FROM HACHETTE INDIA

THE INVISIBLE MAJORITY: INDIA'S ABLED DISABLED

by

C.K. MEENA and V.R. FEROSE

Sixteen fractures and eight surgeries caused by brittle bone disease could not stop Ummul Kher from cracking the prestigious IAS exam and joining the civil services. The determination of homemaker Smrithy Rajesh to educate her child impacted by autism and ADHD empowered her to forge a career path for herself. Inspired by a blind friend, Pancham Cajla successfully transformed several railway stations, making them accessible to the visually impaired. These are only a few of the umpteen stories of resilience, courage and remarkable determination that offer a sensitive, holistic view of the lives of persons with disabilities in this much-needed book for today's India.

Navigating a range of topics with lucid ease – from history and laws to widespread social attitudes – it meticulously records and amplifies the diverse, vibrant voices of persons with disabilities. Equally, it turns its gaze on those inextricably linked to their lives – health professionals, educators, trainers, employers, caregivers and activists – highlighting the key roles they play.

Insightful, informative and moving, *The Invisible Majority: India's Abled Disabled* is a timely and invaluable book that inspires societal transformation while addressing the crucial question: how do we make India a more inclusive nation?

The Autobiography of a Cancer Centre

The Power *of* Hope

ANSHU DOGRA with DR DIGPAL DHARKAR

WITH A FOREWORD BY DR JATIN P. SHAH

MORE FROM HACHETTE INDIA

THE POWER OF HOPE: THE AUTOBIOGRAPHY OF A CANCER CENTRE

by

ANSHU DOGRA with DR DIGPAL DHAKAR

In 1987, Dr Digpal Dharkar, freshly trained at the Memorial Sloan Kettering Cancer Center, New York, dreamt of setting up a world-class institution for head and neck oncology that offered the latest cancer treatment, particularly to the indigent in India, where cancer is the second – and fourth-highest killer of adults across urban and rural areas. With a majority of people in rural areas facing economic difficulties only a few were able to afford cancer treatment and often diagnosis was left until it was too late, leading to unnecessary fatalities. With grave hurdles to overcome and the odds stacked against him, Dr Dharkar summoned his deep resolve – and the commitment of like-minded medical professionals – to establish a charitable trust, the Indore Cancer Foundation (ICF), which would help make a difference in head and neck cancer care in India.

Inspiring and deeply moving, *The Power of Hope* is the compelling tale of Dr Dharkar's journey into the depths of human empathy and a testimony to just how much we can achieve if only we hold on to hope.